# INSURGENT LOVE

# INSURGENT LOVE

## Abolition and Domestic Homicide

Ardath Whynacht

Fernwood Publishing
Halifax & Winnipeg

Editing and text design: Brenda Conroy
Cover design and artwork: Emily Davidson
Printed and bound in Canada

Published by Fernwood Publishing
32 Oceanvista Lane, Black Point, Nova Scotia, B0J 1B0
and 748 Broadway Avenue, Winnipeg, Manitoba, R3G 0X3
www.fernwoodpublishing.ca

Fernwood Publishing Company Limited gratefully acknowledges the financial support of the Government of Canada, the Canada Council for the Arts, the Manitoba Department of Culture, Heritage and Tourism under the Manitoba Publishers Marketing Assistance Program and the Province of Manitoba, through the Book Publishing Tax Credit, for our publishing program. We are pleased to work in partnership with the Province of Nova Scotia to develop and promote our creative industries for the benefit of all Nova Scotians.

Library and Archives Canada Cataloguing in Publication

Title: Insurgent love: abolition and domestic homicide / Ardath Whynacht.
Names: Whynacht, Ardath, author.
Description: Includes bibliographical references and index.
Identifiers: Canadiana (print) 20210260254 | Canadiana (ebook) 20210260378 | ISBN 9781773634838 (softcover) | ISBN 9781773630854 (Kindle) | ISBN 9781773634937 (PDF)
Subjects: LCSH: Homicide—Canada. | LCSH: Family violence—Canada. | LCSH: Homicide investigation—Canada. | LCSH: Discrimination in criminal justice administration—Canada. | LCSH: Police brutality—Canada. | LCSH: Law enforcement—Canada.
Classification: LCC HV6535.C2 W49 2021 | DDC 364.1520971—dc23

# Contents

*For Nora, our early spring crocus.*

*With love for all the impossible, tender things that sprout from the depths of the cruelest winters.*

*With gratitude for R., G., K. V. & S.*

# Preface

On a dark, wet evening in March 2016, I was struggling to light the fireplace when my phone rang.

"It's Kristin," she said. "Kristin is dead."

I paused. My guts went cold. "Have they arrested Nick? Is he alive?"

She gasped for air on the other end of the line, holding back tears so she could speak. "Yes."

❧ ◊ ❧

For decades, advocates who work with survivors of domestic violence have been predicting domestic homicide with tragic accuracy. Those who know *know* when someone's life is in danger. That knowledge can save lives.

Kristin Johnston's relationship should have raised numerous red flags amongst her peers, but no one feared for her safety. Her friends and family recoiled in shock and surprise when her ex-boyfriend took her life. For those of us who are familiar with patterns in domestic homicide, red flags feel like sense memories. It's like smelling something familiar, but you aren't sure where it is coming from or why it makes your blood run cold.

But what are we supposed to *do* when our fears are anchored in experience and our gut is telling us we are in danger?

What do we *do* with that?

Most precursors to domestic homicide are not necessarily criminal, and even when they are, few report the violence and even fewer receive consequences that lead to improved safety. Reporting to police can be dangerous as abusers often retaliate when bystanders or survivors report their concerns to police. Policing, as a general strategy of crime control in contemporary settler states, has not kept us safe from family violence.

I am someone who believes in abolishing police and prisons. Despite working for two decades with survivors of family violence and those who have been convicted of homicide, sexual abuse and intimate partner violence, I don't fear a world without prisons. Working with incarcerated people has given me an intimate glimpse into how—rather than improving community safety—policing, prosecution and imprisonment intensify the cycle of violence and create more dangerous conditions for us all.

Decades of activism, social research and brilliant scholarly work have made a case for abolishing prisons and police to improve safety and bring healing and justice to our communities. Abolitionist feminism seeks to transform the conditions that give rise to violence. Abolitionist feminism acknowledges that intimate partner and family violence cannot be seen as separate from state violence, which arises through the military and police. For those of us who want to see what the world looks like beyond the horizon of what Beth Richie calls a "prison nation," we are indebted to Black and Indigenous feminists and queer, trans and two-spirit organizers, who have shown us a multitude of paths forward.

Yet, despite teaching and writing as an abolitionist, I still found myself perched on the edge of a hard wooden bench in a courtroom pleading for a guilty verdict for a friend of mine who had murdered his girlfriend. Ground zero—the territory in which the impacts of homicide are immediately felt—is ripe with mess and contradiction. As Shira Hassan reminds us, transformative justice "is nothing if not sitting with the beautiful mess" (Dixon and Piepzna-Samarasinha, 2020, p. 203). Thinking through the most dangerous forms of family violence and how we might respond without police, guns and state violence is heavy and hard.

With this book, I wanted to gesture towards transformative justice for domestic homicide. I wanted to start thinking about what an abolitionist strategy for domestic homicide might look like. I don't have all the answers. I share, however, my own journey in thinking through how we can get out of the dead end of carceral feminism and start contextualizing domestic homicide within settler colonialism and racial capitalism. We don't spend enough time thinking about what makes someone a killer. We don't have the right tools for responding to their violence and the risks they pose to our kin.

This book is my attempt to spark a conversation between those who work to understand domestic homicide and high-risk family violence and those who are committed to transformative and abolitionist movements for justice. The prison system should not be our only redress for homicide. I wanted to write something that could help us build spaces of safety and refuge so our movements can be inclusive to those who have been most deeply impacted by ongoing systems of coercion, control and violence. Writing this book is helping me to mend the tear that opened up in the earth beneath my feet on the day that Kristin Johnston died.

In the short period of time between the killing of Kristin Johnston and the final draft of this book, two high profile tragedies occurred in Nova Scotia. In Guysborough County, Shanna, Aaliyah and Brenda Desmond were killed by Lionel Desmond before he took his own life. In the community of Portapique, a mass shooting incident began with an attempted domestic homicide and resulted in the loss of twenty-two lives across Nova Scotia. This was the largest mass murder in Canadian history. These tragedies form the backbone of the story I seek to tell in the pages ahead.

Grappling every day with violence takes its toll. Many of us who make a daily practice of responding to violence in our communities face the cumulative effects of bystander or vicarious trauma. We often turn to this work because of our own experiences with violence, which leaves us processing layers of personal trauma with the effects of frontline work.

During the writing of this book, a period from 2016 to 2020, I became intimately acquainted with a tangled mess of state and intimate terrorism that left me numb and broken. In this four-year span, Kristin Johnston was killed, and I faced constant threats and abuse from trolls in the comment sections of newspaper articles I was quoted in. As a feminist academic who does research on family violence, it is my job to contribute to public discussions on domestic and family homicide. This work comes at a cost. I received countless letters from survivors and perpetrators of domestic homicide after being featured on a national radio show to discuss trauma, stigma and risk factors for violence. On one morning, I arrived at work to a handwritten letter full of intimate details of killing and visceral outpourings of remorse. Someone phoned my campus office to say they were thinking of killing their family. They needed someone to talk to. One of my students narrowly escaped her boyfriend, who became suddenly abusive when she tried to leave the relationship, and I spent nights lying awake, knowing her apartment was on the ground floor and he could easily break the glass and climb in the window.

During Nicholas Butcher's trial for the killing of Kristin Johnston, I sat through every minute of the proceedings. The medical examiner provided detailed testimony of each wound found on her body. We listened to the entire 911 call, where Butcher called for help after cutting off his hand in a botched suicide attempt after the murder. During the trial, a new roommate moved into my house after fleeing an abusive partner, and her ex-boyfriend visited regularly to watch our house from his car on the street. While I worked to process the trial at home in my pajamas, I made sure the blinds were drawn and the dogs were alert in case he was outside, looking for an open window. During this time, every door, every window, every relationship was to a portal to imminent danger.

I still feel that way sometimes. I've felt that way to some degree since I began working with survivors in 2000. It's easy to feel like the world is *naturally* dangerous. It's easy to forget that it doesn't have to be this way.

After a long career of working on violence, trauma and healing, I was numb and withdrawn, battling depression and PTSD, which left me with little capacity to function or feel anything at all. In 2019, I took a break to process the consequences of thinking, breathing and writing about violence every day.

The birth of my daughter forced me to pick up the pieces of my mental health. I returned to this manuscript. Maybe it is more accurate to say that I returned to the world again. I returned to life-sustaining conversations about prison abolition and transformative justice. Feminist abolitionist colleagues and allies made this work seem possible. I felt and still feel a sense of responsibility to the ones who will inherit this broken world of ours.

The generosity of men serving life sentences for violent crimes—their honesty and vulnerability in conversation about these issues—also made this work seem possible. I owe my own healing and the completion of this book to survivors, incarcerated people and activists who are working to build another world with the broken pieces of our carceral state.

I want to stress that my experiences with homicide and intimate partner violence are not an anomaly. Countless frontline workers, volunteers, friends, Aunties and activists face an onslaught of mess and danger as they work to protect the ones they love from family and state violence. This persistent snarl of crisis and violence is a daily reality for many of us. My own experiences as a queer cisgender femme with white privilege are on the gentler end of a spectrum of brutal violence in our communities.

When you speak publicly about the unspeakable, you can become a lightning rod for energy that is already in the sky. Taking a stand against state and family violence comes at a cost. If you are reading this book, I imagine you are standing with us, in the aftermath of such violence, and looking toward a future that is less painful.

Not all survivors of intimate partner violence will agree with what I argue in this book. That is okay. I don't expect everyone to agree with me.

As I worked on this "abolitionist" book, I found myself praying that my friend who murdered his girlfriend would receive a 200-year sentence and die in prison. This shit is complicated.

If you are debating whether you want to dive into a book that spends a considerable amount of time talking about violence and murder, here are some things to consider:

This is a book for those who advocate for survivors of family violence and are willing to question the role of the carceral system in making safer communities.

This is a book for proponents of prison abolition and defunding the police who want to think strategically around managing and reducing the harms of the "dangerous few" who risk the lives of our kin.

This is a book that searches for a way out of existing carceral feminist approaches to domestic homicide.

This is a book for students of transformative justice who want to think more precisely and intentionally around responding to the most dangerous forms of intimate terrorism in our communities.

This is a book written for and with survivors of intimate and state terrorism—who impel us to imagine a world free of police violence and domestic homicide as we build spaces of safety and refuge within our movements.

Thank you for reading this far. Thank you for your willingness to dive into this mess with me. This book is for you, too. I hope you find something helpful in here.

# Domestic Homicide and Abolition

"While prison abolitionists have correctly pointed out that rapists and serial murderers comprise a small number of the prison population, we have not answered the question of how these cases should be addressed. The inability to answer the question is interpreted by many anti-violence activists as a lack of concern for the safety of women."
— Incite! and Critical Resistance, 2001, p. 142

"The stakes, then, are high, when it comes to assessing domestic homicides, phenomena that strike at the heart of how and what it means to get close to others, to build and maintain families and kinship networks (variously defined), to raise new generations, and to contribute in a thoughtful and prosocial way to broader society."
— Neil Websdale, in Jaffe et al., 2020, p. xix

Domestic homicide is the murder of one's intimate partner and/or other family members. "Domestic" refers to the home or family. It is a word we use for the space that contains our most intimate relations. The definition of domestic homicide differs across jurisdictions, but it is generally understood as killing that occurs in the context of an intimate or familial relationship. These tragedies often involve the suicide of the killer and/or the murder of bystanders or witnesses. In countries across the world, death review committees have been established to provide inter-agency analyses of domestic homicide to better prevent and respond to such tragedies (Dawson, 2013). The Canadian Domestic Homicide Prevention Initiative argues that to understand and prevent domestic homicide, we must use a "social ecological model" that is attentive to how risk factors for violence operate at different levels of an individual's experience (Jeffrey et al., 2018). However, despite increasing use of social ecological models and inter-agency death review committees, rates of intimate partner violence remain persistently high and, in times of economic or social stress, are on the rise (Fox, 2004; Lagerquist, 2016). Despite expanding awareness within the violence prevention industry of the need for social ecological models and intersectional approaches to preventing domestic homicide, these tragedies continue to be treated as "anomalies" in an otherwise peaceful society. Collectively, we continue to assume our "domestic" spaces are safe places. Saidiya Hartman (2020) reminds us: "We want to maintain a fiction that desire exists on one hand and violence and coercion on the other, and that these are radically distinct and opposed." Hartman, like others (Davis, 2003; Wilson Gilmore, 2007), argues that intimate violence is normative and embedded in the foundations of the nations that contain us.

For the most part, solutions for preventing domestic homicide are understood in and through state-based systems of policing, prosecution and punishment. Safety is understood as something provided through secure shelters, though they rely on the whims of charitable donors to keep their doors open and never seem to have enough beds for the survivors who need them. It is often cited that *a woman is killed by her partner, on average, every six days in Canada* (Statistics Canada, 2014). As official agencies, consultants and non-profit staff work together to improve public responses through state-funded agencies, we continue to lose women and gender nonconforming people to intimate partner violence at an alarming rate. Those who face the highest statistical risks for homicide and intimate partner violence also face the highest risks for state violence through police, child-protection agencies and prisons (Richardson/Kinewesquao et al., 2017). For those who face state violence through police and prison systems, their experiences with coercion, violence and destruction of autonomy echo throughout public and private life. For Black, Indigenous, disabled women and gender nonconforming people, contact with police poses more danger than an abusive partner.

## Police Homicide

Police are what we call our "domestic security" forces. They are ones tasked with serving, protecting and keeping us safe inside the nation states that contain us. Police also perpetrate a significant number of homicides. Between January 1 and November 30, 2020, police shot fifty-five civilians

(Malone et al., 2020). *Police shot a civilian, on average, every six days in Canada in 2020.* Although the majority of these victims were men, the Women's International League for Peace and Freedom point out that "Black and Indigenous women are significantly more likely to be killed by the police compared to white women" (2021; see also Richie, 2012). Police and military personnel also perpetrate intimate partner violence in their own families at a higher rate than the general population (Macquarrie et al., in Jaffe et al., 2020). Black and Indigenous women have been arguing for decades that intimate partner violence must be understood in the context of ongoing state violence (Davis, 2003; Palmater, 2016).

This book takes this directive seriously. I consider police homicide to be an incarnation of domestic homicide. How can we conceptualize state violence and family violence together as we work to prevent domestic homicide and heal from the tragedy?

## A Note on Language

Many of the pioneers in domestic violence research were feminist frontline workers who were invested in the liberation of women from patriarchal violence. However, in the decades since feminist organizing against domestic violence emerged in the 1970s (Bumiller, 2008; Sheehy, 1999; Richie, 2012), our understanding of the roles of racism, homophobia, class and cisnormativity has complicated both our views on intimate and family violence and our approaches to ending it. Research and writing on family violence are interdisciplinary and involve various and often conflicting political and institutional loyalties. The language we use when we try to understand painful, complex and difficult lived realities for those who experience family violence can carry harmful baggage with it. I try my best to be intentional and clear in how I use language, but at times I may need to use terms that make sense within the work I am discussing.

In the following pages, as much as possible, I refer to intimate partner violence, child abuse and elder abuse by using the term "family violence." "Family" and "family violence" are terms that are usually understood as referring to heterosexual nuclear families. As resistance to colonial Christian conceptions of kinship I use the term "family" to mean to *both* biological and chosen kin (Tallbear, 2018). "Family," in this sense, refers to chosen, biological or legal arrangements between and amongst those who inhabit homes together, care for each other, or engage in romantic or sexual relations. I acknowledge that this is not the understanding that many of my peers in the domestic violence research industry hold, but I am a queer person. My understanding of family is informed by my upbringing by and with my chosen family.

"Intimate partner violence" refers to how we understand violence in an intimate relationship. "Gender-based violence" refers to violence that occurs because of a person's gender. In some ways, this term is more inclusive of transgender survivors of transphobic violence. In other ways, however, it strips the specificity of focus on how intimacy, love and violence can coexist in domestic spaces. Data on "gender-based violence" lumps hate crimes perpetrated by strangers together with more intimate forms of family violence.

Much of what we know about killing within a home or relationship is informed by research on "intimate partner homicide." However, use of this term ignores data that demonstrates that in almost half the cases, the killer attempts or completes suicide (Velopulos et al., 2019). There are often multiple casualties when a coercive partner turns to homicide, including children, elders and bystanders, who are also killed in approximately 20 percent of cases (National Coalition Against Domestic Violence, 2020). So, intimate partner homicide, a term that more broadly encompasses both queer and heterosexual couples, renders invisible the killing of other family members. Child and elder victims are often overlooked in this pattern of violence; young survivors, bystanders and other family members also suffer loss of life (Scott et al., in Jaffe et al., 2020; Websdale, 2010). Each of these terms, in different ways, reflect a frame of analysis that separates the act of killing one's partner from the act of killing one's child and from the act of killing oneself, as if they are all separate incidents.

In this book, I use the terms "domestic homicide" and "family violence" to account for the many survivors and deceased victims of violence in intimate and domestic spaces. After spending decades of my life working with survivors of state and family violence, I no longer see any utility in using frameworks that do not account for the *complexity* of relations between and amongst survivors and victims of lethal family violence. If we accept that the violence in our homes is a microcosm of larger cycles of state violence, then we must use terms that broaden and open up our categories of analysis to account for this.

In this book, "woman" includes both cisgender and transgender women.

There is a strong global movement to advocate for calling every homicide of a woman "femicide" and to track and compile data on the killing of women to account for the gendered dimensions of the crime (see UN Human Rights Office of the High Commissioner, 2021). Social media movements to #callitfemicide advocate for framing the homicide of every woman in the same way: a casualty of men's patriarchal violence. Additionally, a sizable fraction of the research on femicide coming out of United Kingdom is rife with transmisogynist and transphobic hatred. It is extremely difficult to do feminist work on domestic homicide (especially in the United Kingdom and Canada) without coming into regular contact with openly transphobic researchers who often hold high-profile positions in public universities and a considerable amount of power and influence in the field. This needs to change.

Transphobia also represents a glaring problem when it comes to research design and methodology. Queer, trans and two-spirit people are overrepresented in high-risk abusive relationships and, unfortunately, in domestic homicides (National Center for Transgender Equality, 2015; Donovan and Barnes, 2020). Even though queer and trans people are overrepresented in statistics on intimate partner violence, there remains "widespread heteronormativity and cisnormativity" in the field (Donovan and Barnes, 2020). In fact, current research "suggests that the rate of domestic violence is equal or greater than in heterosexual relationships" (Rossiter et al., in Jaffe et al., 2020, p. 65) and that queer and trans people are at greater risk of homicide. Attention to femicide as a "women's issue" does little to acknowledge the intersection of risk faced by queer and trans partners who experience severe relationship violence (Donovan and Barnes, 2020) and homicide.

Another methodological failure of data-tracking movements that simply count and compile data on the killing of *women* is that this approach often fails to account for how men's involvement in the cycle of violence outside the home might impact their use of violence within their own family. It is well known that men are much more likely to be victims of homicide than women. The rationale for counting women's deaths separately from those of men or gender nonconforming folks is "about underscoring that when women and girls are killed, it is in ways that are very distinct from the ways in which men and boys are killed and, therefore, prevention requires an approach that recognizes those differences" (Dawson, in Gerster, 2020).

However, in a carceral society that adopts a black and white, Eurocentric understanding of victim and perpetrator (Russo, 2018), links are rarely made between the killing of women and violence that is enacted upon men, consistently, in work, recreational and domestic spaces as children and youth. Advocacy movements that argue for gender-exclusionary or cisnormative language and frameworks are ill-equipped to provide useful data or perspectives that can inform *prevention*. If we don't understand family violence and domestic homicide in all its complexity, with deep commitments to intersectional dimensions of risk and danger, then we haven't learned much in the last fifty years.

Language is a slippery and tricky thing. I find myself most uncomfortable when using terms to refer to a person who kills, or tries to kill, their partner or children. If you call them a "killer," it is accurate. But it only carries with it one aspect of a person's identity. As an abolitionist, I believe in the power of healing and rehabilitation. I believe that by understanding the experiences of someone who has killed, we can best equip ourselves to heal our communities before tragedies occur. This is why I wince when calling someone a killer, even if they are, because they are, or were, more than that at some point in their life. In a carceral society, it is too easy to discard someone completely and ignore their capacity for change.

My own professional experience with policing and, later, in prisons, has peppered my subconscious with other terms, like "perpetrator" and "offender." These terms make me uncomfortable for other reasons. The professionalization of these terms within the legal system works to distance the person from the visceral act of killing. I often find myself using these terms, but it never feels right. It does not feel right to use terms that distance us from the material and bodily sensations that domestic killing sparks in us. I don't want to naturalize these tragedies or gloss over the graphic reality of the harm. In abolitionist writing, one might encounter the term "person who harms." This, too, never feels right to me. It feels gentle and encompassing to the person who has harmed. It also feels too gentle for describing the person who kills the people they are closest to.

At other times, specific to research on high-risk family violence, I use the term "intimate terrorist" or "coercive partner." These terms are specific to a particular body of work in domestic violence research. I hesitated to use the term "terrorist" as it is often deployed in racist ways that mobilize state violence against racialized people. But the strategic use of violence to create an atmosphere of terror is exactly the type of state and intimate violence that I discuss in this book.

I have yet to resolve my feelings around which terms to use in discussions of killing and those who have killed. I feel that this discomfort comes from living in a carceral society that relies on binary categories of good/evil to avoid any sustained analysis or response to the *causes* of domestic violence. The violence I refer to in this book is almost unspeakable. How do we speak of it and the person who channelled it into the lives of their most vulnerable kin? I caution the reader to avoid taking up these terms in ways that make a neat and tidy box around a killer. These terms should not become labels that allow us to forget about or grieve the person that exists alongside, within and through the killing. We must grieve the person they could have been had they not become a killer.

Through the process of writing this book, I was forced to sit with my discomfort around the labels I used for those who harmed in deep and unspeakable ways. I encourage you, as the reader, to acknowledge, name and give space for any discomfort you might feel, too.

## Feminist Abolition

This book offers a feminist abolitionist perspective on domestic homicide. By abolition, I mean building a world without prisons or police.

Feminist movements against intimate partner and sexual violence in the United States and Canada are relatively new. In her keynote address at the Color of Violence Conference in 2000, Angela Davis (2000) acknowledged: "A little more than two decades ago, most people considered domestic violence to be a private concern and thus not a proper subject of public discourse or political intervention." Early grassroots movements against patriarchal violence called for increased state support to protect victims from abusers who harmed, with impunity, in domestic spaces, which were traditionally considered private and not subject to regulation in the public sphere (Sheehy, 1999; Bumiller, 2008). Since the 1970s, feminist movements against family violence have been increasingly dominated by carceral approaches to social change. A carceral approach to family violence views policing, prosecution and punishment as the primary means of addressing intimate partner and sexual violence (Richie, 2012; Law, 2014; Schenwar and Law, 2020). Second-wave feminist organizing against intimate partner and sexual violence took aim at under-enforcement of laws geared to protect women from violent partners (Kim, 2018; Law, 2014; Bumiller, 2008). In parts of the United States, advocates sued police departments for failing to protect victims of violence (Law, 2014) and, by the 1990s, the largest piece of crime legislation in the history of the United States signified a shift in how family violence would become part of an emerging "law and order" agenda (Bumiller, 2008).

The Violence Against Women Act, or VAWA, is often cited by predominantly white feminist movements as a win in the fight against intimate partner violence in the United States. The VAWA, a legal instrument designed to funnel resources into policing and imprisonment as the primary strategies for responding to family violence, was similar to other strategies employed by second-wave feminist movements to address under-enforcement of laws intended to protect women from violence. In Canada, the Royal Commission on the Status of Women was appointed in 1970 and identified problems with how the laws pertaining to family violence were written into the Criminal Code (Sheehy, 1999). In Canada, much like the United States, women's movements "attempted to introduce formal equality by forcing police, prosecutors and judges to deal with wife assault as they would any other life-threatening harm. However, the demands made by the women's movement have tended to be translated by the state in punitive terms rather than as a way to protect women's lives and safety" (Sheehy, 1999, p. 65). During the 1970s and 1980s, the default solution to patriarchal family violence was to change laws by making sentences harsher and to funnel greater resources into police budgets to investigate and throw offenders in prison.

However, as Alexandra Natapoff (2006) points out, *under*-enforcement and *over*-enforcement are twin problems of a carceral system that excessively punishes Black, poor, disabled and disenfranchised communities and ignores their experiences with violence. Carceral feminism emerged as the dominant voice in organizing efforts against intimate partner violence through the rise of the "prison nation" in the late twentieth century (Richie, 2012). The prison nation reflects the "ideological and public policy shifts that have led to the increased criminalization of disenfranchised communities of color, more aggressive law enforcement strategies for norm-violating behavior, and an undermining of civil and human rights of marginalized groups" (Richie, 2012, p. 3). The new "tough on crime" rhetoric of the late 1980s and 1990s fostered increased collaboration between feminist anti-violence organizers and police (Bumiller, 2008). Beth Richie argues that during this time, the "white feminist anti-violence movement was becoming more entrenched in an overly simplistic analysis that argued that gender inequality was the main factor that motivated violence against women—almost to the exclusion of other factors" (2012, p. 2). This analysis—that men are solely responsible for violence—does not acknowledge the ways in which violent forms of state-building, such as slavery and settler colonialism, have worked to normalize forms of violence and abuse. It absolves white feminists of a need to acknowledge their own complicity in systems of violence. White women in the anti-violence movement, who were less likely to be subjected to police violence or abuse at the hands of state agencies, aligned themselves with the same agencies that waged assaults on poor, racialized and underserved communities, creating a rift in the anti-violence movement. Richie (2012) and others (Davis, 2003; Kim, 2018; Russo, 2018; Kaba, 2020; Kaba, 2021) draw attention to the ways in which carceral feminism is complicit in the very systems it seeks to disrupt by relying on narrow frameworks to understand and address gender-based violence.

Fifty years after the emergence of pioneering movements against family violence, it is safe to say that a carceral approach has failed us. Carceral approaches to family violence do not keep us safer, and, in many cases, contact with police and the court system causes more violence for survivors, who often face mistreatment at the hands of police and prosecutors (Ryan et al., 2021). Incite! and Critical Resistance (2001) point out: "Law enforcement approaches to violence against women *may* deter some acts of violence in the short term. However, as an overall strategy for ending violence, criminalization has not worked." Mandatory arrest laws, which force police to lay charges where warranted (regardless of consent from the survivor) have led to increased criminalization and incarceration of survivors (Law, 2014; Kaba, 2021; Ryan et al., 2021). This means that those who engage in self-defence to save their own lives or those of their children may face jail time (Kaba, 2021). Carceral feminism "conveniently ignores the anti-violence efforts and organizing by those who have always known that criminalized responses pose further threats rather than promises of safety" (Law, 2014). White feminist movements that are aligned with the same systems that abuse Black and Indigenous women betray the origins of feminist organizing. Black feminist organizers, through their experiences with the state and its systems of violence and exploitation, inherently understand the failure of carceral approaches to ending violence.

This, of course, is a condensed version of how and why mainstream (read: white) feminism became complicit in the rise of the prison nation and systematically ignored the violence experienced by Black, Indigenous, queer, disabled, femme and gender nonconforming people, to the detriment of all our safety. For deep and sustained analysis on the relationship between anti-violence movements and the state and why an abolitionist perspective is key to ending gender-based violence, I invite the reader to close this book and, instead, open up the work of Angela Davis, Beth Richie, Michelle Alexander, Mimi Kim, Mariame Kaba, Ruthie Wilson Gilmore and Mia Mingus, among others. Organizations such as Incite!, Generation Five, Philly Stands Up and the Bay Area Transformative Justice Collective have crafted excellent analyses about the relationships between state and intimate violence and highlighted the role of the prison system in maintaining cycles of violence in the United States. For deep analysis on how racism and state violence have persisted in Canada, Robyn Maynard's work (2017) is a brilliant introduction to violent histories of anti-Blackness in settler Canada.

Canada is also a prison nation. Although the federal and provincial prison systems remain partially run through the public sector, many of the problems identified by Black abolitionist feminists in the United States exist in Canada. The globalization of anti-Black racism (Bashi, 2004) and expansion of neoliberal capitalism (Wacquant, 2009) have created similar forms of carceral violence in much of the Western world. In Canada and beyond, legal reforms have served as the official means with which to secure increased safety for survivors of family violence (Fraser, 2014), to the exclusion of Black, Indigenous and other racialized women and gender nonconforming people, who face increased violence and criminalization through contact with police (Abraham and Tastsoglou, 2016). Maynard traces the deep history of anti-Black racism in Canada, pointing to the way in which "Black women and other gender-oppressed people are not only over-policed, but are also enormously under-protected" (2017, p. 153). She highlights a history of racism in violence-against-women organizing in Canada, demonstrating how state funding and complicity with police and prison systems work to alienate Black women, who face high rates of both state and intimate partner violence.

Despite consistent support and funding for policing and punishment in Canada, rates of intimate partner and sexual violence remain high (Statistics Canada, 2014). Indigenous women are six times more likely to be victims of homicide than white women (Statistics Canada, 2014), and Black women continue to face elevated risks for both police (Maynard, 2017; Women's International League for Peace and Freedom, 2021) and intimate partner violence (James, 2007). Vicki Chartrand (2019) argues that the carceral system in Canada represents a continuation of colonial logics and practices that function to undermine the autonomy and sovereignty of Indigenous Peoples. Violence through contact with police and in the prison system is a continuation of historical settler violence that began with the first incarnation of what is now the RCMP (Gouldhawke, 2020). Police homicides account for an average of thirty deaths a year, with Black and Indigenous Peoples facing disproportionately high risks for homicide by police, and emerging data points to an increase in police-perpetrated homicides in Canada over the last twenty years (Singh, 2020). Montreal-based Third Eye Collective (n.d.) emphasize "that strategies designed to combat sexual and domestic violence must be linked to strategies that combat police violence, hate violence, as well as anti-Black, racist, colonial, and anti-immigrant violence that persists against our communities." Given the persistent failure of carceral feminism in Canada to meaningfully engage with those at highest risk for severe violence and death, through both intimate partner and state violence, a need for feminist abolitionist organizing on domestic and state-sanctioned homicide is clear.

## Positionality/Complicity

I am no stranger to policing. In 2001 I took my first real job, as a Victim Services counsellor in a city police unit. As part of this civilian unit, I responded on scene to offer crisis support and referrals to victims of domestic violence. I was the youngest person in the unit by at least a decade. I was also afraid of cops. The summer before I started in the unit, I saw at least half a dozen cops beat a skinny teenager and throw him into the back of a paddy wagon at an anti-globalization protest. I joined the Victim Services Unit to try to confront my fear of cops. It bothered me to think that survivors of sexual assault and family violence were exposed to police during times of intense vulnerability and crisis. I grew up outside of Toronto, and I remember how terrified my mom would be every time she was stopped by an officer with 52 Division. I remember how her voice would tremble, how it felt like we were in danger every time an officer would approach our car. My childhood friends and their families felt the same way. I wanted to support victims of family violence. I didn't want cops to be the only ones who show up when someone had been harmed. My time with Victim Services served as my introduction to feminist politics and the complexities of family violence.

During my first summer at Victim Services, we launched a pilot program to reduce risks for intimate partner homicide. It was the called the "high-risk protocol" for identifying and coordinating cases that appeared to be at high risk for homicide. I helped by filling out questionnaires designed to assess a woman's risk of being killed by her partner. Police in many jurisdictions continue to use versions of this questionnaire, based on the work of Jacqueline Campbell et al. (2003). If a survivor was deemed at high risk for homicide, their case was handled by a special coordinator, who took targeted measures to improve their safety. Risk factors for intimate partner homicide were well-known, even twenty years ago, and this program aimed to use statistical evidence to save lives. When there was police intervention for a "1049," or domestic violence call, we made contact in person or via the telephone to encourage the survivor to access safety resources. In cases with repeated violence, we tried to talk survivors into leaving their partner. This was wildly ineffective. Most, if not all, of the survivors I spoke with during my time at Victim Services did not want to end their relationship with their abuser.

Following my time in the Victim Services Unit, I began teaching in the federal prison system while I completed my PhD. I worked with offenders in the maximum security and structured living units of a women's prison and with men serving life sentences in a federal facility. We met regularly to chat, write poetry and share. Many of the prisoners I worked with over the course of several years in men's and women's prisons were convicted of domestic homicide.

After working with survivors and later perpetrators, I came to call myself a prison abolitionist. After handling multiple calls from the same home over and over again in policing, I knew how difficult it was to convince survivors to leave an abusive partner. After working in a prison system that was a barren wasteland with few rehabilitation programs specialized for intimate partner or sexual violence, I felt that the system was so deeply implicated in a cycle of trauma that it often did more harm than good. Even if someone who was violent *wanted* to take accountability and be rehabilitated, the supports were just not there.

When a high school friend of mine killed his girlfriend in 2016,[1] I felt as if I was trembling at the edge of an enormous chasm. By that time, I had trained for fifteen years as a family violence and community safety "expert" and had spent years of my life learning from those who survived family violence and those who were locked up for killing the ones they loved. Just a couple of weeks before Kristin Johnston's death, I had expressed to a mutual friend that Nick should contact a local men's counselling program that specialized in domestic violence intervention. There was no history of violence in Kristin Johnston's relationship with Nick Butcher—at least, not that we knew of. Still, I had a familiar and nagging feeling in my gut. He was deeply depressed and unemployed, and his relationship seemed to be on the rocks. His friends were worried about him. I suspected that he was a danger to himself *and* his partner.

My warning that Nick might be dangerous was swallowed up in the distance between those who understand that violence is the normative condition of our lives and those who believe that violence is perpetrated by stereotypical villains in places far from where we live and play. My suggestion to bring Nick to a program for intimate partner violence went unheard. Nick couldn't be dangerous—he was just a regular guy. A friend. He was part of our circle. We aren't people who dance with monsters. We are the good ones. I was, as was usually the case when I would raise a point deemed to be "too feminist," dismissed.

As Ann Russo points out, we "tend to divide people into two distinct and rigidly defined subject positions—victim or perpetrator" (2018, p. 22) and place ourselves in the category of innocence. This binary thinking, pervasive within settler cultures that adopt the Eurocentric concept of the world as comprised of pairs of opposites, works to distance us from violence and to evade personal accountability for the ways we have been complicit in harm. This is true of racism, homophobia and misogyny and during instances of extreme violence, such as the killing of Kristin Johnston. The shock and surprise felt by those within her closest circles betrayed the truth of their complicity. Many had known that he was reading her private messages. His closest friend had joked with him about killing her dog as revenge for her suspected infidelity. His circle of male friends, who for decades had made misogynistic jokes and quietly avoided discussing sexual assault and other forms of violence prevalent in their intimate social circles, all processed their grief and bewilderment as if the sky had fallen without warning.

But there are always warnings.

Feelings of shock, betrayal and surprise make sense if you believe that domestic homicide is a rare and random act rather than an all-too-common outcome in a settler culture whose very fabric is held together by coercive control, a desire to "possess" and market forces that "dispossess" us at every turn.

## Healing Justice Has Always Been Here

Abolitionists speak often of transformative justice (Kim, 2018). Transformative justice seeks to transform the conditions that made harm and violence possible. Mimi Kim points out: "Restoration implies the desire to return to such conditions, transformation requires moving beyond" (2018, p. 227). Restorative justice seeks to restore conditions that were altered by an act of violence or harm. Transformative justice heals the wounds that caused the harm in the first place.

Transformative justice has always been an Indigenous practice on the territory I call home. I live in Mi'kma'ki, the unceded territory of the Mi'kmaw People, a place once governed according to Mi'kmaw legal orders, which enacted justice in forms that pre-existed and continue to defy the carceral state my ancestors forcibly imposed upon this land. These concepts belong to the Indigenous worlds that continue to exist despite settler attempts at erasure and carceral state violence.

Practices of restorative justice, adopted from traditional Indigenous practices, have been co-opted and implemented within settler justice systems (Kim, 2018; Nocella, 2011). In much early Canadian abolitionist writing, the terms restorative justice and transformative justice are used interchangeably (Morris, 2000; Lockhart and Zammit, 2005). Movements for transformative and restorative justice often fail to acknowledge the Indigenous or diasporic origins of many of these practices (Withers, 2014). Aileen Moreton-Robinson (2015) writes of the "white possessive logic" that characterizes settler colonialism. This possessive logic of ownership emerges through practices of attribution and citation, which work as a "mechanism of settler-colonial erasure and possession of Indigenous knowledge[;] attribution is a technique of ownership in that it signifies an authorial relationship" (Andersen and Christen, 2019, p. 116). So, while transformative justice is a central political commitment of this book, I want to assert that this concept is not my own and express a commitment to acknowledge its origins in the Nations that grant me continued access to their territory. Although it is beyond the scope of this book to explore the full origins of restorative justice and transformative justice and their relation to Indigenous justice systems and legal orders, I must acknowledge the role that settlers have historically played in ignoring the origins of Indigenous concepts and practices.

In white counter-cultural movements, there is a tradition of romanticizing and co-opting Indigenous customs (Hahn, 2014). This approach to engaging with Indigenous cultures, although it is often framed as progressive or "alternative" to mainstream values, constitutes a perpetuation of white supremacy and settler colonialism. Stereotypes of the "ecological native" (Gilio-Whitaker, 2017) in environmental justice movements or appropriation of Ayahuasca rituals and "shamanic" practices by settler "wellness gurus" (Amor, 2019), to give just two examples, demonstrate the pervasiveness of white supremacy in counter-cultural political movements. Abolitionist movements, specifically white anarchist social movements, have also participated in the theft and co-option of Indigenous forms of transformative justice (Withers, 2014).

Ruth Morris, a leading figure in the Quaker feminist movement in Canada, was a well-known advocate for prison abolition in the late twentieth century. Morris, credited with the origin of the term "transformative justice," writes that the first step toward abolishing prisons and embracing transformative justice is taken by "going back to Indigenous cultures, which recognized the importance of a healing process that would strengthen the whole community, heal the victim, and find a way to reintegrate offenders" (2000, p. 113). While she acknowledges that these concepts are borrowed from Indigenous cultures, there are problems with how the possessive logic (Moreton-Robinson, 2015) of white supremacy continues to erase the origins of the practice. Attribution of the term "transformative justice" to Morris constitutes erasure of Indigenous Nations and a continuation of colonial practices that co-opt, de-politicize and claim authorship over Indigenous land and knowledge.

AJ Withers (2014) points out that casual reference to Indigenous origins of what many of us call "TJ" (transformative justice), or healing justice, imposes pan-Indigeneity on Indigenous communities, which is deeply problematic because it ignores important cultural and political differences between Indigenous Nations. As Leah Lakshmi Piepzna-Samarasinha (Dixon and Piepzna-Samarasinha 2020) points out, there is a harmful tendency to assume that by practising forms of transformative justice within abolitionist movements, we can somehow reverse colonialism completely. As a settler and a writer who seeks to contribute to ongoing discussions about the need for transformative justice, I must commit to naming and acknowledging the ways that white supremacy operates through practices of citation. We cannot fix violence in our communities by stealing Indigenous concepts, claiming them as our own and reinstalling these practices inside our current colonial projects. We cannot return to a precolonial utopia. We must *transform*, rather than restore, our conditions.

We can build transformative cultures in allyship with Indigenous resurgence without co-opting Indigenous forms of healing justice. L'nu legal scholar Tuma Young writes on the need for a restoration of Indigenous language systems and stories to revive L'nu legal traditions:

> Respectful examination of the worldview of the L'nu and other Indigenous peoples is a crucial step in the de-colonization process. Both the dominant and the oppressed culture need to heal from the devastating effects of racist imperialism. Such healing will prove elusive absent reclamation of the L'nuwey worldview and language. One key way to rebalance the relationship is to reincorporate traditional L'nuwey legal principles into contemporary legal praxis and institution building. Such a radical and daunting shift will require deep changes in how knowledge and reality are constructed and experienced. (2016, p. 82)

Young is pointing out that we must address the wounds of colonialism by making space to repair and heal the cultural practices that have been under attack for hundreds of years. To heal from the effects of racist imperialism, L'nu worldviews, languages and practices must be restored. Without this step, we cannot collectively heal from the effects of colonialism.

The globalization of restorative justice principles by settler-state and non-governmental institutions demonstrates the way in which Indigenous healing principles have been selectively co-opted and de-politicized on a global level (Tauri, 2016; Withers, 2014). This is harmful not only because it signifies the ongoing erasure of Indigenous Peoples through colonialism and the imposition of pan-Indigenous stereotypes on multiple nations and cultures, but also because it works to prevent Indigenous Nations from practising their own forms of justice. Indigenous Peoples continue to be disproportionally incarcerated despite inclusion of restorative justice practices in the legal system. In other words, "the extent of Indigenous influence in the design of specific Restorative Justice (RJ) programs has been greatly exaggerated" and "the inter-jurisdictional transfer of these programs has impeded the ability of Indigenous peoples to strive for a measure of self-determination in the Justice sphere" (Tauri, 2016, p. 46).

White-dominated social justice movements that seek to soften the effects of colonial violence and violent crime cannot possibly implement transformative healing practices in meaningful ways unless the worldview, values and cultural fabric of Indigenous communities remain intact. Furthermore, radical concepts and terminology from social movements are taken up by those with institutional power and white privilege, reduced to credentials that can be provided (for a fee) through de-politicized webinars or university classrooms. As Mariame Kaba points out, it's important to strategize against "the RJ [restorative justice] thing, where everybody is now taking circle training, and, as a result of that, they think they know everything they need to know about RJ" (in Dixon and Piepzna-Samarasinha, 2020, pp. 207–28). We cannot reduce transformative justice to a set of credentials or dogmatic politics that ignore the origins of the concept or the de-colonizing commitments it requires of us.

As a settler living on un-ceded Mi'kmaw territory, it is my responsibility to carry these troubling settler histories with me and continually interrogate my own relation to Indigenous cultures and wisdom. In my attempts to radically imagine a world free of domestic homicide, I must acknowledge that practices of transformative and restorative justice that emerged in Canada in the 1980s through the work of Christian feminist abolitionists were *stolen* from Indigenous peoples. The possessive logic of white supremacy (Moreton-Robinson, 2015) facilitates this ongoing theft of Indigenous practices and traditions even in radical spaces.

As we fumble toward worlds beyond the destructive machinery of racial capitalism and settler colonialism, the labour of giving birth to a different kind of future is ours to bear. As settlers, we must stop the continued theft of land, resources and traditions from Indigenous Peoples and do the grinding, sometimes spirit-breaking, work of containing the harms that

and other racialized communities face cycles of violence in their intimate lives that are exacerbated by state violence and intensify through the expansion of the carceral system (Maynard, 2017; Richie, 2012; James, 2007). Although rates of domestic homicide in Canada and the United States have decreased since the 1970s, recent research demonstrates that "domestic homicide [in the US] has increased each year between 2014 and 2017 from a death toll of 1875 in 2015 to 2237 deaths in 2017" (Jaffe et al., 2020, p. 2). Although "domestic homicides appear to be the most predictable and preventable of all homicides" (p. 2), state- and community-based responses are often limited to domestic homicide death review committees only after someone has been killed. Domestic homicide, as it is often referred to, kills approximately 82 women per day and accounts for one in eight homicides globally (Jaffe et al., 2020).

It is important to note that this form of lethal family violence comprises a much higher proportion of homicides in "developed" nations, such as Canada, the United States and the United Kingdom. Domestic homicide claims the lives of children, bystanders and elders. It also afflicts same-sex partners. In some cases, rates of domestic homicide are statistically higher in same-sex relationships than in heterosexual relationships: "Between 2009 and 2017, there were 36 homicides in Canada involving same-sex partners, representing 5% of all intimate partner homicides over this time period" (Jaffe et al., 2020, p. 7). This points to a problem in attempting to contextualize lethal family violence as "femicide," where men's violence against women is the only frame in which causes and solutions are offered. The data on domestic homicide clearly shows that the threat of violence is real and not overblown. Dismissing our fears of the "dangerous few" works to conceal the pervasive violence faced by Black and Indigenous women and gender nonconforming people at the hands of their partners.

As Morris points out, "the once-in-a-lifetime stress murderer who kills his/her own family is the most common type of killer outside of the military" (2000, p. 102). But embedded in the abolitionist claim that we should not fear homicide is an acknowledgement that domestic homicide is a real and present danger. Alternatively, Dana Cuomo (2020) argues that abolitionist movements must pay closer attention to high-risk forms of intimate partner violence rather than relegate them to a footnote in our story about the violence inherent to prisons. Cuomo suggests that renewed attention to misogyny is one way to address the dangers of high-risk intimate partner violence. Although it is important to acknowledge and combat patriarchy and misogyny, simple reliance on these explanations for severe family violence re-assert universalizing and essentialist ideas about men's predisposition to violence; they also work to conceal the ways that racial capitalism and settler colonialism exert occupying forces in our hearts and minds, legitimizing structures and processes of coercion in the settler state.

Taken together, intimate and state terrorism comprise the greatest threats to the safety and security of all of us but more specifically, BIPOC (Black, Indigenous, people of colour), femmes and mentally ill, poor and chronically marginalized people, who are most often targets for police violence and most often neglected by agencies that provide supports for those living with intimate terrorists. As Critical Resistance and Incite! (2003) argue, there is a need to build coalitions for increased safety that do not rely on carceral solutions to danger. We must acknowledge that the "dangerous few" are many and multiple, and we must make space for new and better resources on how to think through abolition and domestic homicide.

In the following pages, I grapple with the failure of carceral feminism to provide meaningful analysis on the connections between ongoing state violence in settler colonialism and domestic homicide. I make these arguments in and through my own experiences as a frontline worker with survivors and convicted perpetrators and through my own journey, as an abolitionist feminist, during the murder trial of my friend. With attention to critical writing on settler colonialism and racial capitalism, I make links between established typologies of intimate partner violence most commonly associated with domestic homicide and strategic colonial policies that legitimate coercive control relations as an ongoing process of settler colonialism in Canada. I argue that domestic homicide finds its origins in the coercive control tactics of the settler state, which planted the seeds for particular kinds of subjectivity through racial capitalism, where the forces of occupation render us vulnerable to existential insecurity and the cold brutality of market forces.

Occupational stress is a major risk factor for domestic homicide. I discuss occupation as a conceptual territory in which we might explore an abolitionist agenda for transforming the conditions that lead to domestic homicide. Occupation, as the ongoing project of colonial state-building in the United States and Canada, relies on a toxic relationship between masculinity—how it is taught and maintained—and the existential impacts of our daily occupations in the global capitalist marketplace. Occupation, as the architecture of our subjectivity in contemporary capitalism, is the space in which we must extricate ourselves and nurture self-understanding and resistance against the forces of work, and colonialism, in our collective lives.

Through autoethnographic reflection and field notes from a murder trial, I explore what it might mean to abolish police and prisons in light of persistently high rates of domestic homicide in Canada and how we might think about the origins of violence differently as we consider transformative solutions. In the final chapter, I look at what this might mean for community-level transformative justice projects that respond to family violence. I reflect on how we might foster insurgent collaboration across rural and urban communities and between and amongst survivors and those who have harmed. Crucially, I explore how we might nurture love and kinship that resists, rather than enables, the relations we are forced into through forces of colonial state-building.

The goal of this collection of personal reflection and post-carceral imagining is to develop an abolitionist position on domestic homicide that takes our safety seriously. When our prison systems are so overcrowded with members of our community who are incarcerated for non-violent crimes that could have been prevented through better funding of addiction and mental health services, it is easy to forget that there are some incarcerated people who are tremendously dangerous to our individual and collective safety. Kristin Bumiller writes that, with regard to "violent crimes against women, it is difficult to imagine policies that would not ultimately rely upon the carceral capacities of the state. Clearly, there are some instances of grave harm that require the segregation of offenders for the protection of society" (2008, pp. 115–16). However, a socio-historical consideration of domestic homicide, rather than serving as a caution to our abolitionist imagination, makes the strongest case for abolitionist strategies to defund, disarm and dismantle the prison system.

## Note

1.  For more information on Kristin Johnston and the circumstances of her death, see Allison Saunders, "Remembering Kristin Johnston," *The Coast*, March 28, 2016 <https://www.thecoast.ca/halifax/remembering-kristin-johnston/Content?oid=5299433> and *CBC News*, "Nicholas Butcher found guilty of second-degree murder of Kristin Johnston,"April 28, 2018 <https://www.cbc.ca/news/canada/nova-scotia/nicholas-butcher-found-guilty-of-second-degree-murder-of-kristin-johnston-1.4640038>.

# Butcher

I met Butcher in high school. We had people in common.

Like so many friendships that began in Halifax, our overlapping circles came and went through various phases of living in Montreal or Toronto, our shared friends making the inevitable pilgrimage to bigger cities and returning again.

Our crew had that waspy thing, that kind of soft-misogyny—you know, that vibe that feels progressive but is underpinned by a deep distrust and hatred for women? The kind of scene where tomboys ran the show, all of us drinking in jeans and t-shirts in somebody's basement, seemingly equal until some dude's feelings got hurt and he turned into a raging misogynist for a bit. Then nobody talks about it.

Drunk cliff-running was a thing. The post-Jackass "let's tie this curbside sofa to the back of a Jeep and ride it" kind of scene. I learned how to aim a saltshaker at someone's eye. Mischief and injuries. And too much alcohol.

Most of the women I shared this time with were queer and in various stages of owning this publicly. It was fine to be queer, as long as you were a girl. I remember how that kind of homophobia felt in the back of my throat.

In truth, I loved them all very much. Every one of those misogynistic assholes. I can't say that Butcher was even the most misogynist. He might have come in at a distant third or fourth place for that title.

I got good at ghosting when things took a turn. Everything was fun until one of us broke someone's heart and we all fell through the ice back to the 1950s.

I was lucky to have places to run to when it felt gross with them. I am lucky to still have some of those people in my life.

❧ ◈ ☙

Butcher was the kind of guy who would quietly fill up a dog's empty water bowl at a house party and then sit cross-legged on the floor, giving a loving ear scratch after calling the pup over for a drink. He was a gentle guy.

His self-presentation shifted completely when he got into law school. Dress shirts and a new ride. I remember barely recognizing him after the transition to white-collar manhood.

I made fun of him. This I remember. Twice, he had dated my closest friends. Twice, he had left them feeling confused and humiliated after a short-term tryst. This was my excuse for being shitty to him, I suppose.

I remember walking down a dark driveway on my way to a party and stumbling into an intense conversation between Nick and Kristin in the shadows beside the house. I didn't know they were dating.

They left holding hands that night.

≈◊≈

It was common knowledge that Butcher was struggling to find work after graduating from law school. He was working at a friend's café and trying desperately to secure an articling position.

Friends testified at the trial that he was hundreds of thousands of dollars in debt. He had a lot of job interviews, but none ended in an articling position.

He was falling apart.

Kristin's friends and family testified at the trial that she wanted to leave the relationship.

Some of Nick's friends knew that he was reading her private messages. There were times when he knew where she was and who she was with even when she didn't tell him.

His friends were worried about him.

We should all have been worried for Kristin.

≈◊≈

The court heard testimony that pieced together the evening before and early hours of March 26, 2016.

We heard that Kristin had been chatting with friends on Messenger about ending her relationship with Butcher. We heard that she was thinking about leaving the province to be closer to family.

We heard Crown evidence that someone had been accessing and reading her private messages from her laptop at Kristin's shared home with Butcher while she was out that evening, using the app on her phone to chat with friends.

Later that night, after sharing drinks at a bar with friends, Butcher found her at another friend's home long after the bars had closed.

Butcher let himself into a stranger's apartment to look for her. One of Kristin's closest friends talked about hearing footsteps in the kitchen before realizing it was him.

Friends testified that he argued with Kristin after entering the apartment in the middle of the night. She eventually agreed to leave and go home with him. This was the last time she was seen alive.

The medical examiner testified that she died as a result of ten stab wounds to the neck. She had defensive wounds on her hands. She was found in her bed, presumably attacked while asleep or lying down.

You can hear Butcher's voice on the 911 recordings.[1]

"I need help—I am dying—I cut off my hand"

"I killed my girlfriend—she's dead"

"I killed her, then I tried to kill myself"

&#8766;◊&#8765;

In controlling, abusive relationships, risk for domestic homicide skyrockets when the survivor tries to leave. Unemployment—especially sudden or unexpected financial or occupational stress—is also a major risk factor for domestic homicide. I had worked in the field long enough to know this.

But from what we know, from testimony and long conversations with friends, there was no point in Kristin's relationship with Butcher where police could or would have intervened prior to the murder.

The rage, shame and distress that Butcher was likely experiencing was repressed deeply enough to prevent him from being openly violent enough to warrant a criminal charge.

Everyone was worried about *him*.

That's the irony, though, right? Men in patriarchy accrue so much "power," but they are often enabled by friends and family who absolve them of accountability. They are absolved of accountability by their loved ones because they see how men are wounded by other men and systems of violence. Butcher's self-esteem and financial future were decimated by a cut-throat job market. We feel pity. We let them off the hook.

Pity is the gateway to so much violence.

Despite ticking most of the important boxes in a domestic violence homicide risk assessment questionnaire, without a criminal charge, police could not have intervened in the points leading up to the murder. Without a history of violence in the relationship, Kristin likely did not believe she was at risk.

⤞◇⤝

Some of us met for drinks at the end of the trial. A few of us had been feeling like we wanted to clear the air between us.

There had been a lot of shit said through the course of the trial and since the murder, and some of it needed to be addressed.

"we don't know that he killed her—let the trial determine whether he is guilty"

"yeah, but she was cheating on him—he must have snapped"

"I feel so sorry for him—I should have been there for him—I am so worried about him in prison"

Those who responded to the killing through misogynistic layers of denial or dismissiveness or by minimizing his accountability did so in full view of those who called Kristin one of their closest friends.

Domestic homicide hits in our most intimate spaces. Where surviving friends and family call the killer their kin. We grieve the killed and the killer together. Every stage of grief is complicated by our relations with both partners. Every stage of grief is mediated by layers of carceral thinking that prevent us from acknowledging that monstrous acts can be committed by people who are not monsters. We flail about in disbelief, seizing onto simplistic explanations.

"he snapped"

"he didn't get the support he needed"

"he was suicidal"

But most suicidal people don't decide to take those they claim to love the most with them into the forever.

I live-tweeted most of the trial with feminist commentary. I passive aggressively tweeted some of the fucked-up comments I had heard leading up to and during the trial. I could barely look most of my friends in the eye, yet I found myself in that familiar all-night diner at the end of the trial surrounded by some of Butcher's closest friends.

A friend took a seat across from me at a long, lacquered pine table. VLT machines flashed behind us. The server brought a few pitchers of beer to the table.

"we need to talk"

He's angry that I've been tweeting about how many of our friends have been behaving as if Butcher is the victim.

He accuses me of lying. He doesn't believe that any of our friends still support Butcher. He has been living in Australia the last few years. He could not have been farther away from what was happening as grieving friends and family came to terms with the killing, yet somehow, he is absolutely sure that everyone is on the right side of history. He can't and won't believe that anyone in our circle might be misogynistic in any way.

All of our relations have become a snarl of anger and feelings of betrayal.

I remember pulling my coat on quickly as I left.

⧖◇⧗

There is a paper I often use when teaching about masculinities with my students. Michael Flood, an Australian masculinities theorist, did a study with young men at a military academy (2007). He draws upon Sharon Bird's notion of homosociality (1996) to explore how men's bonds with each other shape their sexual relationships with women. His interviews with the young men in the study are disturbing. They joke and laugh in violent ways about women. His paper forced me to think through how a lot of the violence we experience as women and femmes is mediated by men's social relationships with other men.

⤜◇⤛

I cried when I drove home that day from the bar. That friend who accused me of being a liar was one of Butcher's closest friends. I don't understand how he could have been so close to him for so long and missed the warning signs too. Sometimes we think that friends and family can help us be accountable. But other times it seems like we're trapped in ecosystems of enabling toxic guilt and shame.

A guilty verdict was not going to heal our relationships. A guilty verdict was not going to take the pain away from Kristin's surviving family. A guilty verdict was not going to force Butcher to atone for his sins.

A guilty verdict was not going to address or heal any of the harms done by years of misogynistic violence in our shared social circle.

A guilty verdict will not address the impunity that some of his closest friends continue to grant him.

Butcher was one of a long lineage of dangerous guys in our inner circle.

The sexual assaults by that same dude they kept inviting back to future events, on overnight canoe trips... Everyone knew about that. No one cared enough to intervene or protect their friends from him.

The physical assault that left a friend with a bruised face, and Butcher's good friend who knew about the assault but still hosted the abuser's art show a couple of months later as if nothing had happened.

The women who acted like Butcher was the true victim on the day he killed Kristin. The ones who cried as if they were the victims when they saw him, pale and withdrawn in the courtroom.

None of this will heal the social context that excused decades of brutal misogyny.

⤜◇⤛

I am a few weeks pregnant with my daughter at the sentencing hearing. I arrive late because I was throwing up in the courthouse bathroom. My pants are already too tight, and it hurts to sit on the wooden bench in the back of the courtroom.

I don't have a lot of faith in the courts. Myrna Dawson's research (2015) demonstrates what she calls an "intimacy discount" in sentencing for domestic homicide. She argues that women—wives and romantic partners—are still seen as property. This explains why men who kill women they are close to receive lighter sentences than those who kill strangers.

Butcher's ex-girlfriends are testifying for the Crown at the sentencing.

Kathleen recounted a story about how, after her breakup with Butcher, he claimed he was doing well in his PhD program and convinced her to let him come visit. When he showed up to her apartment early, he somehow bypassed the building's security and came straight to her apartment door without buzzing in.

She testified that he searched through her bathroom garbage can. When he found used condoms, he became agitated and frightened her. She discovered that he had been reading her private messages and emails. She testified that he had spat on her during their relationship. She said she regretted not reporting this to police at the time.

When he came for the post-breakup visit, he admitted he had not been doing well. He was staying in his room for days, smoking cigarettes. She testified that she began to fear for his safety and for her own. She testified that, after contacting his mother, he was admitted to a psychiatric facility in Montreal.

I find myself wondering how many times he had come close to killing after a breakup.

I find myself wondering how many other women's garbage cans, email accounts and Messenger accounts he had been rifling through in the years I knew him.

In a victim impact statement, Kristin's mother said she fears for her safety when Butcher is eventually released. I heard the same from some of my friends.

A sentence is nothing but a temporary reprieve from the nightmare of footsteps on the kitchen floor.

⁂

After the trial, I meet up with a friend for a walk on the beach. We talk about the day I suggested Butcher needed to go to a men's program for domestic violence.

I talk about my deep regrets in not communicating my fear more assertively to others. At the time, I wasn't close enough to Kristin to call her directly to express my fear about her relationship. I am angry with myself that I hadn't communicated a sense urgency as I remember the deep sense of dread I felt when I realized he was in mental health crisis while his career was falling apart and his girlfriend was about to leave him.

She says she never suspected violence. But she recounts, in intricate detail, the day she saw them sitting together at a friend's cottage. He had his arm around Kristin's shoulder, tightly, as everyone wandered around chatting and laughing in the sun.

Kristin was not a wallflower. She was funny and boisterous and badass. She ran her yoga classes like she ran her business—with strength and focus.

"There was something about the way he had his arm around her that day... It was too close—he was holding her too close—like he owned her"

## Note

1. Excerpt of 911 call played at Nicholas Butcher's murder trial, Canadian Press. <https://www.youtube.com/watch?v=k4-cUsLOTDg>.

# Settler Colonialism and Intimate Terrorism

"We have said before, and we say again, if it is sickness you seek, don't look for it in the victims of genocide: it resides in the minds and hearts of the people who planned, designed, implemented, and operated the machinery of genocide."
— Roland Chrisjohn and Sherri Young, 1997, p. 126

"Assault is an essential part of this strategy and is often injurious and sometimes fatal. But the primary harm abusive men inflict is political, not physical, and reflects the deprivation of rights and resources that are critical to personhood and citizenship."
— Evan Stark, 2009, p. 5

"In premodern settings we find no trace of the mass killing of a spouse or partner and one or more of their children."
— Neil Websdale, 2010, p. 216

It's 1841. A gentleman with sideburns and a neat combover stands in front of a lecture hall of eager students at Oxford University in Britain. Professor Herman Merivale is an expert on colonial policy, specifically, how to secure the cooperation of settlers in generating surplus wealth for the Empire. In 1841, Canada was a British colony. Colonizers were particularly concerned with how to keep British citizens loyal to the Empire once they settled into the Canadian wilderness and became self-sufficient. On this particular day, Merivale is delivering a lecture titled "The Political Relation of the Colonies to the Mother-Country" to a group of eager students hoping to find work in the administration of the colonies. He looks out from the podium at the faces of his students and begins:

In the colonies; every thing which adorns human life, every thing which stimulates the more artificial appetites of men, be they sensual or spiritual, is either difficult of acquisition or unattainable. The colonist has little temptation to long for the enjoyment of such superfluities; for the stimulus of envy is wanting: he does not see them heightening the pleasures of others and therefore thinks little of them. During the first period of his conflict with the genius of wilderness, his thoughts are necessarily intent on immediate employment; afterwards, his daily labour for ordinary comforts is sufficient to occupy the common faculties of body and mind. He is in danger, therefore, of sinking into a state of listless and inglorious indolence—a state in which whole communities may vegetate on an extensive surface, raising little surplus wealth, and each generation contenting itself with the habits and enjoyment of that which preceded it. To counteract this tendency, he has only what may almost be termed the abstract desire for accumulation. I mean, the desire for the amassing of wealth, unconnected with the passion for its enjoyment. (1861, p. 613)

Merivale is telling his students that to prevent settlers from becoming content to homestead on the lands they occupy, they must nurture "the abstract desire for accumulation." This desire, as he puts it, must be "unconnected with the passion for its enjoyment." The settler must be trained to desire the accumulation of wealth but must never actually *experience pleasure or contentedness* with what they have. Desire must be disconnected from pleasure, completely. If the settler becomes content to homestead and raise a family in the colonies, they will stop generating surplus wealth for the Empire. They stop seeking to amass more and greater resources. But Merivale says one can never possess enough; the consumer drive to possess more and greater material goods must define the settler's very reason for being. The settler must work and never stop working to amass wealth for the Crown.

Domestic homicide is a consequence of this desire for accumulating objects, which never leads to enjoyment. This toxic relationship between masculinity, work and Empire is one that bleeds over into domestic life in tragic and terrible ways today.

Current trends in domestic homicide can be traced back to the emergence of the nuclear family during early colonial periods. British colonists brought the legal practice of coverture to the Americas, whereby the rights of the wife became subsumed by her husband through marriage (Berkin, 2017). Colonialism introduced to the Americas the idea of women as "chattel," or property, of their husbands (Stretton and Kesselring, 2013). Although relationship violence exists in many cultures and periods of history, the most dangerous form of relationship violence that leads to domestic homicide is an outcome of European colonialism.

Domestic homicide arises from a particular type of relationship that is characterized by "coercive control" (Stark, 2009), or "intimate terrorism" (Johnson, 2008). In these highly dangerous intimate and familial relationships, the abusive person feels overwhelming possessiveness toward their partner. The abusive partner in a high-risk abusive relationship views their partner as an extension of themselves rather than as an autonomous being (Auchter, 2010). Aileen Moreton-Robinson points out that "there are inextricable connections between white possessive logics, race, and the founding of nation-states" (2015, p. 13). White supremacy in settler colonial states, she argues, is defined by a patriarchal "possessive logic" that facilitated theft of land from Indigenous Nations and persists today through processes of ownership, entitlement and objectification. These processes of "ownership, entitlement and objectification" are the products of colonial policies executed by Herman Merivale and his contemporaries. The extension of the logic of ownership and objectification of land and life unfolded through the enslavement of Black Africans in the Americas, where Black people were treated as commodities that could be bought, sold and violated with impunity (Hartman, 1997; Maynard, 2017). Leanne Betasamosake Simpson urges us to think about colonialism as a "structure of processes" and connects the dispossession of land and bodies with ongoing destruction of Indigenous sovereignty: "Land and bodies are commodified as capital under settler colonialism and are naturalized as objects for exploitation." She argues that "sexual and gender violence has to be theorized and analyzed as vital, not supplemental, to discussions of colonial dispossession" (2017, p. 41). The origins of patriarchal possessiveness (Moreton-Robinson, 2015; Stark, 2009), colonial dispossession and lethal family violence must be understood as a recent historical phenomenon, a result of the extension of British patriarchy to secure settler participation in emerging capitalist orders.

Connections between patriarchal violence and the objectification of women are not new. Feminist critiques of the patriarchy have identified the role of objectification of women as a means with which to possess, violate and kill women (Dworkin, 1974). Catharine MacKinnon similarly defined patriarchal objectification as "when a human being, through social means, is made less than human, turned into a thing or commodity, bought and sold" (1987, p. 173). Possessive logic is also what drives many abusive partners to kill. However, carceral feminism works to conveniently forget the white supremacist origins of men's lethal violence against their kin and naturalizes men as inevitable threats to women's safety and security. Carceral approaches ignore their collusion with the very same systems of state violence and dispossession that created the violence in the first place.

This chapter argues that the first formations of coercive control relations in the Americas were those of the colonial administration with Indigenous Peoples. Historical and present-day colonial processes, which foster "possessive logic" and depend on discouraging the experience of pleasure by promoting the abstract desire for wealth, serve as correlating and motivating factors for an "intimate terrorist." For example, early colonial police forces utilized "strategic" and tactical violence to secure broad control over Indigenous territory and Nations. These same forms of violence have been identified as correlating factors in relationships that have ended in domestic homicide. Domestic homicide is a contemporary expression of strategic colonial policy, which nurtured "possessive logics" in racial capitalism through the nuclear family. After six generations of settler colonial policy, most, if not all, of us embody the logics and emotional styles of racial capitalism. Colonial architecture, engineered by colonizers like Herman Merivale, is alive and well inside those who transgress terribly through the annihilation of their families and often, themselves.

## Typologies of Intimate Partner Violence

Not all instances of intimate partner and family violence are the same. Most intimate partner violence does not end in homicide. There are distinct trends and patterns in how different abusive relations unfold in intimate and familial relationships. We can think of these types of violent relationship as different dances—distinct choreography that is performed to the same patriarchal melodies but offering vastly different patterns of movement. In *Decriminalizing Domestic Violence*, Leigh Goodmark points out that intimate partner violence "ranges in seriousness from pushing to homicide, making it difficult to target specific behaviors for prevention" (2018, loc. 1568). Goodmark argues for a decriminalization perspective that uses a public health approach to understanding differing causes of violent behaviour. This approach, she believes, will be more effective than current carceral approaches, which render the causes of violence irrelevant in a court of law. Carceral approaches to intimate partner violence are limited by the narrow scope of the Criminal Code and offer punishment rather than rehabilitation.

However, there is also a tendency in critical feminist and abolitionist writing about violence to flatten all experiences of violence and treat them with the same broad strokes. Yasmin Nair (in Warren and Nair, 2016) argues that when we work to trace the origins of gender violence back to everyday practices and structural processes, we may inadvertently de-legitimate lived experience of a bodily assault. Abstract theorizing about gender-based violence may be necessary to understand how violence is taught and maintained, but all too often we see "differing instances of sexual aggression, violence and assault flattened into a concept [such as rape culture] that leaves little room for nuance or particularity, perhaps more importantly, so are those who are the subjects of such violence" (Warren, in Warren and Nair, 2016). Abolitionist strategies for responding to and preventing domestic homicide must be attentive to the particular forms of violence that give rise to killing. Some forms of relationship violence can be dealt with through community accountability circles (Creative Interventions, 2012; Dixon and Piepzna-Samarasinha, 2020), but other forms of family violence are too dangerous for a one-size-fits-all approach to building safety. Shira Hassan points out: "We need to address that violence differently" (in Dixon and Piepzna-Samarasinha, 2020, p. 201).

Risk factors and patterns associated with domestic homicide are well-studied (Campbell et al., 2003; Dawson, 2013; Jaffe et al., 2020). To understand patterns of *relations* that give rise to persistently high rates of lethal domestic violence, we must be attentive to patterns and trends in intimate partner violence and acknowledge established risk factors. One of the biggest risk factors for lethal family violence is what Michael Johnson (2008) and others (Stark, 2009; Crossman et al., 2016) deem a pattern of coercive control or intimate terrorism within an intimate partnership or family network. In the following section, I review Johnson's typologies of intimate partner violence with specific attention to what he calls intimate terrorism or coercive control relationships. An abolitionist consideration of different types of family violence demonstrates how the most lethal form of family violence replicates patterns of coercive relations that emerged as a result of settler colonial policies and the formation of the nuclear family, ultimately leading to the prevalence of domestic homicide in everyday life.

## Intimate Terrorism and Domestic Homicide: Johnson's Typology

For years, family violence clinicians and feminist researchers were divided on the role of gender in intimate partner and family violence. Numerous studies (Steinmetz, 1977; Kurz, 1989) refuted the claims of feminist researchers that men were more likely to engage in intimate partner violence.

By the mid-nineties, Michael Johnson, a sociologist with expertise in domestic violence, offered another framework for understanding family and intimate partner violence. In his original study (1995) and later book (2008), Johnson argues that there are four distinct types of intimate partner violence: intimate terrorism (or coercive control), situational couple violence, violent resistance and mutual violent control. He argues that "intimate terrorism," the most dangerous of his proposed types, was the type of abuse most often seen by shelter workers and women's advocates in community-based social service agencies. This type, according to Johnson, is seen most often in the shelter system as severe abuse by cisgender men in heterosexual relationships. Another type, "situational couple violence," represents a large number of violent relationships where power imbalance is not so distinct between the two partners and where both partners can engage in boundary-crossing or aggressive behaviour, even when there is an imbalance of power.

Johnson believes that discrepancies between the claims of feminist domestic violence experts and family violence clinicians could be resolved by acknowledging that they were each seeing drastically different forms of violence:

> My feminist approach, rather than seeing all intimate partner violence as involving a general pattern of control, distinguishes among types of violence on the basis of the control context in which they are embedded. Intimate terrorism is violence embedded in a general

pattern of coercive control. It is the violence that we encounter most often in shelter populations, in emergency rooms, and in law enforcement. In heterosexual relationships, it is perpetrated almost entirely by men, and it has been the basis of most feminist theories about the nature of domestic violence. It has a completely different dynamic than does situational couple violence, a type of violence that is not about general control, but comes from the escalation of specific conflicts. (2008, pp. 2–3)

Johnson argues that an understanding of the context of control and power in the relationship can help us to understand what type of intervention is most appropriate; a narrow focus on specific acts of violence, rather than on their effects in the context of the relationship, ignores important details relevant to our understanding of risk and prevention. The type of abuse in the relationship can be understood not by how frequent or severe the violence is but by understanding violence as part of a larger strategy of eroding the autonomy of the survivor to maintain control over them. In this sense, "intimate terrorism is violence embedded in a general pattern of coercive control" (p. 2).

Violent resistance, the second type of intimate partner violence, is a relationship in which an intimate terrorist seeks to maintain control through coercive means, but the survivor engages in violence to resist their control. Mutual violent control is a relationship in which both partners use coercive control measures against each other; this type is exceedingly rare. The most common type of violent relationship, situational couple violence, can be understood as a high-conflict relationship where both partners are likely to have trauma histories, addiction issues and/or attachment wounds and where boundary-crossing or aggressive behaviour is common as an escalation of conflicts.

It is important to note complexity within this typology: there can be power differences in situational couple violence and the violence can be severe or even fatal, and intimate terrorist relations can be free of physical violence, something that Johnson refers to as "incipient intimate terrorism" and others call "nonviolent coercive control" (Crossman et al., 2016). Coercive control can be maintained through financial, verbal or psychological forms of abuse. A survivor of intimate terrorism may experience stalking and surveillance without direct forms of physical aggression from their partner. As Johnson points out, in intimate terrorism, "violence is not all of it" and "not the worst of it" (2008, p. 13; see also Dobash and Dobash, 1979).

When we speak of the connections between family violence and state violence, it is important not to flatten all forms of family violence into a single layer or use abstract notions of "violence" to make broader points about power and injustice. Johnson's (2008) and Stark's (2009) descriptions of intimate terrorism name the type of violence that is most likely to that lead to homicide, which is a pattern of relations that echo the ways in which settler states secured nationhood through the violent dispossession of land and life. Johnson's analysis of situational couple violence names and describes the forms of family violence that emerge due to trauma histories or attachment struggles between and amongst partners and kin. Not all forms of family violence manifest patterns of state violence in the same way. Johnson's typology provides a framework for understanding power and risk in family violence intervention and allows communities to triage their energies towards the protection of those who are in the most danger.

While I was attending Butcher's trial, I rented out a room in my house to a new roommate. She installed light-blocking blinds on every ground floor window the day she moved in. Cheyenne worked as a continuing care aide and was rarely home.

After a few weeks of living together, I noticed an SUV with tinted windows parked across the street from our home every evening. Ours was a dead-end street with half a dozen houses. A neighbour asked me if I knew the person who would park and sit inside their truck every night. I shook my head.

Eventually he made his way to our door with a bouquet of flowers for Cheyenne. He was tall and wearing a brown leather jacket that smelled like cigarettes. He had the body language of a shy toddler meeting a new adult for the first time. He was soft spoken and earnest. He asked if she lived there. I said yes.

Within a few days, the police would be in our dining room taking both of our statements.

He was her ex-boyfriend. She left him with only the clothes on her back and was in hiding from him. He found her by following her car home from work.

She was panicking. She was terrified.

He was sending her declarations of love and begging her to return. He made a scrapbook of "their love" and left it at her work. She had blocked him online, but he made new accounts and used new email addresses every time she blocked him.

I told her this is why I have dogs. I assured her he wouldn't get past the front door before they would fly into a loud and snarling rage, alerting the household. I convinced her to always leave via the front door, where the neighbours could see her and where he had nowhere to hide if he was lying in wait for her.

I convinced her to call the cops.

I sat with her, re-filling her mug of tea, while she showed the messages and flowers to the fresh-faced cop who took up half the space in the room. He said the messages appeared to be non-threatening. He didn't think there was an issue. He suggested that she call the anti-cyberbullying unit and ask him to stop.

He said the street was public, and he couldn't ask him to stop parking in front of the house. He told us there was no crime. He couldn't understand why a bouquet of flowers left her so terrified that she couldn't eat or sleep.

The second time we called the cops, I did all the talking. I demanded to speak to a staff sergeant. I peppered my language with references to pro-arrest policies and the high-risk protocols, and I remained standing as I told the cop that I was working in his station before he had even graduated from police college. I directly quoted—from memory—the definition of harassment in the Criminal Code. I was on the offensive.

Cheyenne said little. She had detailed everything in a notebook. She was tired of explaining herself over and over again because the officers who showed up didn't put their notes in the DACT system properly after the last call.

She was already making plans to leave the province. He had multiple registered and unregistered firearms. She told me he kept a hunting rifle in his SUV.

I thought about how police found a sharp kitchen knife in the front console of Butcher's car after the night he killed Kristin.

Cheyenne moved out shortly after. The cops eventually charged him. I was subpoenaed as a witness for the Crown, but Cheyenne had disappeared long before the trial. The prosecutor wrote and asked if I knew her new address, or how they could get in touch with her. I had no idea.

I never heard from her again.

## Intimate Terrorism/Coercive Control

Intimate terrorism is the type of abusive intimate relationship that is most likely to end in homicide. A coercive control relationship, defined by acts of intimate terrorism (physical or non-physical), is the type of violent relationship that many of us think of when we think of an "abuser." This type of relationship has been the focus of feminist activism, media attention and public advocacy over the past fifty years. In a coercive control relationship, a survivor is not free to leave (Stark, 2009). As Johnson and others note, a survivor often has no access to money or supports that would give them the autonomy to leave the relationship if they fear for their life. Those living with a coercively controlling partner know that risk for violence will escalate when they express autonomy, make social connections outside their relationship or do anything to threaten the illegitimate claim of their partner to their body and spirit. Those who find themselves in a coercive control relationship are not likely to be an active part of community mobilizing or be regularly present for movements for social justice or community change. They are the ones who quietly disappear from their social networks, often for years at a time.

Intimate terrorist violence works strategically to reinforce non-physical control strategies. Within a coercive control relationship, the damaging effects of "ostensibly nonviolent tactics that accompany that violence take on a new, powerful, and frightening meaning, controlling the victim not only through their own specific constraints, but also through their association with the general knowledge that her partner will do anything to maintain control of the relationship, even attack her physically" (Johnson, 2008, pp. 8–9). Threats of violence work to maintain a stable pattern of control that gives an intimate terrorist unfettered access to the physical and emotional resources provided by their partner. An intimate terrorist seeks security by restricting, dominating and occupying their partner's very existence, using a wide range of tactics that degrade and destroy the survivor's sense of self. Violence exists to reinforce a pre-existing set of relations enacted through forms of abuse that function together to keep the survivor in the relationship. An intimate terrorist often threatens children, family members or pets as a way to control their partner's behaviour. Survivors know that leaving this kind of relationship can be fatal.

Whereas situational couple violence is characterized by violent acts in the context of specific arguments between a couple, in a coercive control or intimate terrorist relationship, "contingent violence; i.e., violence enacted as punishment for a failure to comply with the explicit or implicit demands" (Johnson, 2008, p. 14), is used strategically to enforce compliance with the desires of the violent partner. In an intimate terrorist relationship, surveillance becomes a necessary strategy for an intimate terrorist to maintain control over their partner's behaviour at all times. This includes snooping, stalking or the use of technology such as apps or home alarm systems to monitor the survivor's every move. This kind of surveillance is also prevalent in policing strategies to enact terror in Black communities, using carding (Mukherjee and Harper, 2018), street checks and "stop and frisk" (Stop Police Terror Project DC, 2021) to create an atmosphere of fear and a sense of being watched.

More important, however, is a subtler form of manipulation that works to erode the autonomy and desire of the survivor to "call their life their own" (Johnson, 2008, p. 15). Legitimation, or the process of convincing a survivor that the intimate terrorist has the *right* to enforce demands upon them, requires an erosion of the partner's sense of self, trustworthiness or sanity. The intimate terrorist's control over their partner often extends to household finances (Stark, 2009), leaving survivors unable to pay bills or feed themselves if they step outside the reach of their coercive partner. Intimate terrorism in a relationship means that there is a much higher risk for domestic homicide.

## Situational Family Violence

Most intimate partner violence is not intimate terrorism. Most abusive partners do not engage in a wide range of coercive control tactics. Situational couple violence is the most common type of violent relationship. Although situational couple violence can be dangerous and, in some cases, fatal, it is not characterized by continuously escalating violent episodes, coercion, surveillance and a pattern of seeking control over the survivor. Couples may fight about issues related to jealousy or control in the relationship, but each conflict is not necessarily connected to a broader pattern of coercion, surveillance, legitimation and gradually decreasing autonomy of the survivor. The importance of distinguishing between situational couple violence and intimate terrorism lies in our ability to intervene safely, prevent homicide or suicide of the abusive partner and provide community-based interventions that are specific and relevant to the abuse or violence taking place in the relationship.

Some research demonstrates that situational couple violence is more common in communities facing multiple and overlapping facets of oppression from white supremacy, economic marginalization or colonization (Johnson, 2008). Additionally, the presence of misogynistic attitudes in the relationship is not correlated with an increase in or severity of aggression in situational couple violence. The same research shows that the damaging effects of structures of oppression and marginalization do not increase risks for intimate partner terrorism or coercive control relationships. Another major difference in correlating factors between situational couple violence and coercive control is that intimate terrorists are more likely to hold misogynistic or patriarchal attitudes toward women or femme-identified people. Understanding differences between situational couple violence and coercive control, as defined by Johnson and others, allows us to be attentive, with care and specificity, to the various types of relations that are produced in response to chronic stress, structural oppression and childhood abuse and neglect. It also allows us to trace where specific forms of state terrorism are being employed strategically in intimate partnerships.

The usefulness of these typologies of family violence lies in their ability to tell us when and how we can intervene safely when folks in our community need our help and which tools we should use when we intervene. Broadening our collective literacy in patterns in family violence allows us to conduct our own risk analysis so that communities can respond safely to both high- and low-risk forms of family violence without police intervention. This is explored more fully in the final chapter.

## Rigid Typologies Are Always, Unavoidably, Imperfect

There is danger in strictly applying Johnson's typology to all experiences of intimate partner and family violence. One danger is that the damaging effects of situational couple violence might be minimized or dismissed as compared to the homicide risks associated with coercive control relationships and intimate terrorism. Typological frameworks are useful for movements for prison abolition and healing justice only insofar as they are used pragmatically and with critical attention to what they *miss* as well as what they may *capture* in their descriptions. Johnson's typologies and concepts of coercive control are relatively new, and experiences of intimate partner violence, specifically in LGBTQIA2S+ relationships and nontraditional blended or polyamorous relationships, are not always captured in mainstream research on intimate partner violence.

Although family violence researchers in this tradition have made important contributions to our understanding of the micro-relations of intimate terrorism, they have largely failed to provide intersectional analysis that draws connections between overarching systems of white supremacy, which are founded on illegitimate occupation of territory, pervasive anti-Blackness and strategic neglect that unfairly distributes precarity and abuse to those who might disrupt a stable pattern of coercive control in the settler state. Johnson and others seek to build a feminist sociological understanding of intimate partner violence in the context of control patterns, but literature on intimate partner violence often overlooks the tremendous analytical insights provided by Black and Indigenous feminists who are attentive to intersectionality and the role of multiple and overlapping systems of oppression and violence in our intimate lives.

Nevertheless, careful attention to differences in types of intimate partner violence yields important insights into how communities can respond to various and differing types of violent relations outside of the carceral system. Johnson's typology, read in and through Black and Indigenous feminist work, points to an important distinction between those who engage in violent relations due to a lack of coping mechanisms or as a reaction to acute stress and those who engage in violent relations strategically through coercive control in order to maintain illegitimate claim over their partner's agency. Situational couple violence, as described by Johnson, offers an opportunity for community intervention and healing justice approaches that can reduce relationship violence and support both partners in improving their sense of safety and security in their relationship. Understanding differences in violent relations offers a threshold for which forms of community accountability and healing justice are safest and most effective. Additionally, Johnson's (2008) and Stark's (2009) descriptions of coercive control and intimate terrorism provide a basic framework for understanding how some forms of intimate partner violence echo the strategic use of state violence through the ongoing project of settler colonialism.

## Settler Colonialism, Policing and Homicide

It is true that most family violence in Canada is the result of stress, traumatic experiences and/or mental health or addictions related issues. It is also true that the rarer, more *dangerous,* type of intimate partner violence echoes patterns of early colonial violence and control over Indigenous territories. This pattern of strategic, coercive means of securing possession of territory, eroding the autonomy of others, surveillance and legitimation of this violence is characteristic of an intimate terrorist in an abusive relationship that is high-risk for domestic homicide.

Familicides, specifically, have roots in early settler colonial state-making and the emergence of the nuclear family. Critical historical attention to trends in domestic homicide demonstrates that prior to colonization, there was no record of a pattern of family-killing in the Americas (Websdale, 2010). Understanding domestic homicide beyond what Roland Chrisjohn and Sherri Young (1997) call "methodological individualism" in colonial scholarship, which positions violence as arising from the individual rather than their culture, requires us to tune into the "structures and processes" (Simpson, 2017) of colonial violence that exist today. Policing is one of these ongoing processes of colonial violence that draws upon the same patterns of coercive control seen in high-risk intimate relationships. Vicki Chartrand traces the history of colonization to the contemporary penal system in Canada, drawing upon Foucauldian notions of "episteme" to describe the processes by which colonial logics persist in the structures and processes of colonialism today:

> An episteme can be traced through a history of the present that reveals how historic processes have discursively emerged into specific logics—or modes of reasoning—that we continue to cultivate today. A logic of colonialism emerged within modern narratives of

progress that made the containment, segregation, assimilation, and elimination of entire populations a central feature of its organizing practices. (2019, p. 71)

If we understand coercive partners and contemporary police forces to pose twin threats to the safety and security of our shared communities, then we can more clearly grasp approaches to domestic homicide that account for how it is taught and perpetuated in everyday life.

❧ ◊ ❧

Kelly is a survivor of intimate partner violence. Her husband was a cop and they lived in the town where he worked.

When she called the police on her husband, his co-workers and friends were the ones who responded.

She told me that she felt manipulated into saying particular things in her statement to police. She felt like they covered things up so her husband wouldn't get in trouble.

So, she decided to become a cop and try to turn that corruption around.

"I really came to the conclusion that people like me should get into policing: People that can be objective, that have integrity, that are honest, and that wouldn't stand up for a friend in a case like that. They'd have to do what they thought was right. So, it was shortly after that that I started the process to get into policing, and it was the year after that I was hired and started my job with Waterloo Regional Police."

We are sitting in an empty classroom at Humber College after a symposium on transformative justice hosted by a local non-profit organization that works with survivors of child sexual abuse.

Kelly is the kind of person you want to show up if you are trouble. She is kind and confident. She exudes a calm energy and has razor sharp analysis of power dynamics at work in every space she is in. Her body language is firm and strong. She can read body language and the affect of a room in seconds. I feel safe with her.

She tells me about how, after a few years with her regional police force, she began to notice how officers at every level were covering up intimate partner and sexual violence perpetrated by their peers.

She tells me about a friend of hers who was dating a cop in her unit. After trying to end the relationship, he stalked her. Kelly's friend was so frightened that she slept in the attic of her home at night. She slept there because she could pull the attic stairs up and lock them from the top, so he couldn't climb up to reach her. He broke into her home. He sent frightening messages and harassed her from his police cell phone.

Kelly tried to take this to her supervisor. They shut her down. She went over her chief's head to the Police Services Board.[1]

Instead of responding to her complaint about an officer on the force harassing and threatening his ex-partner, Kelly was informed that she is "being investigated" for allegedly violating the Police Services Act. They tell her she is not allowed to communicate any further with the Police Services Board. They make her life miserable at work. She is put on desk duty.

Her union is not helpful. Kelly tells me that the cops who aren't bad apples are terrified of the ones who are. No one is willing to stand with her to address cops who perpetrate intimate partner or sexual violence on the force.

She doesn't give up.

"I was on a mission to just research and find out, how do they get away with this? And what can be done to bring this to everybody's attention? So, as I was researching, I started writing, and I ended up finding all these cases where they had done the exact same thing to other people. So, I ended up writing a research paper that was half about the abuses of power that are done in policing and the other half was done about how the system silences police whistleblowers. When I say the system, it's because, you know it's not just the police services with their punitive action, but it's when that officer reaches out to all these other agencies that should be intervening, nobody does. And it's almost like there's just this inherent trust because of the status and authority that these police chiefs have."

She becomes an advocate for better whistleblower legislation in policing.

She starts working with a coalition of community groups, including survivors of police violence, for police reform legislation in Ontario. The legislation was hamstrung when the Ford government was elected in Ontario.

She tells me that she feared for her life when she went public about corruption in the Waterloo Regional Police Force. She's been diagnosed with PTSD.

I ask her if, given her experiences fighting corruption in policing, she thinks we should abolish the police. She shakes her head. She shrugs. She believes that every community needs someone to turn to, someone with integrity and good training, who can help them when they are in trouble.

She talks about how important community-based safety work is. She talks about how every time she was in a school, working with kids, she would scan the doors and the layout of the building and plan for an active shooter scenario.

In her mind, the problem is with government and the public. Neither seems to be interested in limiting or reducing the power of police. Neither seems to want to exert authority over police chiefs. She sees the problems in policing as an extension of those same problems in society.

If we live in a culture dominated by misogyny and abuse of power, and people have access to firearms, then someone's gotta respond to an active shooter, right?

☙ ◈ ❧

Policing in Canada began with colonialism, where armed, mounted officers were tasked with forcibly protecting the expansion of colonial powers (Palmater, 2020; Gouldhawke, 2020). In the late 1800s, Canada "desperately needed a paramilitary police organization to enforce its new oppressive laws, the Dominion Lands Act of 1872 and the Gradual Enfranchisement Act of 1869 (later updated as the Indian Act in 1876), which were designed to control Indigenous peoples and redistribute their lands to settlers, in violation of the Numbered Treaties" (Gouldhawke, 2020). Policing in the colonies took a very different form than policing in Britain (Walcott, 2021). Early colonial police forces were used to wage a campaign of terror against Black and Indigenous Peoples (Saleh-Hannah, 2015; Maynard, 2017). For communities that were historically treated as a threat to colonial expansion and control, police represent the very same expressions of violence that they claim to protect us from.

Carceral feminist strategies for reducing domestic homicide perpetuate the myth that organizations like the RCMP can be collaborators in our endeavours to end gender-based violence. The persistent myth of the benevolent Mountie works to conceal the gendered and racialized violence that police perpetrate every day:

> Conventional Canadian mythology maintains that the RCMP was created to protect Indigenous people from marauding Americans at Cypress Hills. But even this whitewashed story underlines the force's role in expanding and maintaining the borders of Canada while facilitating the development of infrastructure such as the Canadian Pacific Railway across Indigenous lands by whatever means necessary, from forcibly relocating Indigenous people to breaking workers' strikes. (Gouldhawke, 2020)

Coercive control was, and continues to be, the primary means of policing in settler colonial states. Carceral feminism's ongoing relationship with policing betrays the truth of its complicity with terror in both state-sanctioned police violence and intimate violence.

Uncritical collusion with the police in movements against family violence represents an extension of the colonial project; it perpetuates the racist myth that police keep us safe from family violence. Pam Palmater (2020) argues that the RCMP have always existed as the violent arm of a colonial state for the purpose of surveilling, controlling and terrorizing Indigenous Peoples. This recognition of the connection between early colonial history and present-day patterns of police violence extends to those who work within the carceral system for settler colonial governments. In his *Report on the Independent Police Oversight Review* (2017) in Ontario, Justice Michael Tulloch identified a need to acknowledge the historical role of police as "agents of colonization responsible for controlling Indigenous peoples."

For those who have worked in police oversight, historical legacies of policing present a barrier to effective police reform. In a tell-all book about corruption in police oversight bodies and the struggle for police reform in Toronto, former chair of the Police Services Board Alok Mukherjee and journalist Tim Harper point out that Black residents in Toronto continue to face abuse at the hands of the police: "Blacks were considered property in Canada well into the 1800s, and a United States slave patrol law allowed Blacks to be pursued and monitored to the Canadian border during that time" (2018, p. 197). Mukherjee and Harper see police reform as a strategy that is doomed to fail because the racist legacies of chattel slavery and colonial terror continue through corrupt and abusive forms of contemporary policing. We need abolition and transformation. We can't hold abusers accountable unless we understand the roots of their behaviour and can acknowledge and name their violence with clarity and precision. This applies equally to police and to abusive family members and partners.

## An Abusive Relationship with the State

Police perpetrate violence in gendered and racialized ways. For example, in Val d'Or, Quebec, an investigation by Radio Canada uncovered a series of sexual and physical assaults perpetrated by police officers on Indigenous women (Page, 2018; Canadian Press, 2016). A neighbouring police force was brought in to investigate and uncovered "38 cases of complaints of police abuse, including rape, sexual assault, harassment, and so-called 'starlight tours,' where police would allegedly take people against their will and drive them far outside town and abandon them" (Canadian Press, 2016). This is just one example of many. Sexual assault and family violence perpetrated by police are not a new phenomenon (Palmater, 2016; Macquarrie et al., in Jaffe et al., 2020). Since their inception, colonial police forces have waged a campaign of gender-based violence against Black and Indigenous women (Saleh-Hannah, 2015; Maynard, 2017). The racial and gendered dimensions of police brutality are well known and not limited to the United States and Canada (Amnesty International, 2021; Vitale, 2017; Maynard, 2017; Richie, 2012; Mukherjee and Harper, 2018).

When we apply Johnson's (2008) and Stark's (2009) research on types of family violence to the relationship between the state (including police as the state's enforcement arm) and Black and Indigenous Peoples, it becomes clear that this is a severe and high-risk form of violence and that it is a manifestation of strategies used by colonial regimes to enslave, dispossess and control the population. In both forms of terrorism—state-sanctioned and intimate—we see violence used strategically to politically erase the autonomy of survivors, the use of surveillance to create an atmosphere of fear and the use of physical violence and other forms of coercion to force compliance. The state's pervasive patriarchal tendency to treat women and racialized and Indigenous Peoples as objects to "possess" (Moreton-Robinson, 2015) began with European colonialism, where in "its forced labor branch of chattel slavery, land and bodies alike were simultaneously transformed into conquered properties" (Saleh-Hannah, 2015). In this sense, we can see both police and intimate partner violence as an extension of treating others as property to be controlled, exploited and possessed. Beth Richie (2012) points out how Black women across the United States face the dual impacts of police and family violence. Expanding the frame of analysis to address violence against those who were the targets of historical colonial violence shows the pattern of police violence carrying over into other state agencies and into domestic and intimate spaces. Many women experience family violence while living in community and then experience an extension of the same pattern of violence and coercion inside prisons. Palmater writes:

> The over-representation of Indigenous women and girls that are murdered or disappeared at the national level is significant, but some of the provincial statistics present a much darker picture as Indigenous women and girls represent 55 percent of all of the women and girls that are murdered or go missing in Saskatchewan and 49 per cent in Manitoba. They are three times more likely to suffer violence and significantly more likely to be killed by an acquaintance than Canadian women. While domestic abuse is part of the story, Indigenous women are less likely to be killed by a family member than Canadian women, so this factor is not the whole answer. (2016, p. 255)

Palmater argues that homicide statistics should be compiled in ways that include deaths in custody and at the hands of state officials with data on intimate partner homicide. After all, Palmater argues, Indigenous women's organizations have compiled data demonstrating that "prostitution is not a cause of murder, that not all women are killed by their spouses, and that the causes included violence at the hands of state officials, such as death in police custody" (2016, p. 256).

Understanding the risks faced by those who are over-represented in homicide statistics requires us all to expand our analysis beyond a simplistic understanding of patriarchal violence and account for the ways in which gendered state violence is enacted in public and private life. When police are perpetrators of gender-based violence, they cannot be the solution to it (Davis, 2003). Alex Vitale (2017) and Alok Mukherjee and Tim Harper

(2018) argue that the answer to police-perpetrated violence is not reform; it is an abandonment of our current practices and a courageous reconsideration of what it means to keep each other safe. As Macquarrie et al. (in Jaffe et al., 2020) argue, the culture of policing and military institutions echoes a culture of coercive control that is seen in abusive relationships. In this sense, police must be understood as state-sanctioned intimate terrorists as they routinely engage in patterns of public and private violence in the patterns identified as coercive control abuse. They must be defunded, disarmed and abolished.

## The Nuclear Family Is a Microcosm of the Settler State

Those who face the highest risks of death from police-perpetrated homicide or domestic homicide at the hands of their loved ones are those who were historically treated as chattel, or property, either through slavery (Maynard, 2017; Saleh-Hannah, 2015), colonization (Moreton-Robinson, 2015; Simpson, 2017) or marriage (Stretton and Kesselring, 2013). An ancestral history of being treated as property to be owned and abused translates to present-day risk for domestic homicide at the hands of loved ones or police. This history of objectification and dispossession of land and life by European colonists is recent and coincides with the emergence of family-killing, or familicide, as seen in contemporary life. It also includes attention to how the legal institution of marriage and incarnations of the nuclear family worked to render women "non-persons" under the law, subject to their husband's will and authority (Stretton and Kesselring, 2013; Berkin, 2017).

Although it is beyond the scope of this book to offer a comprehensive history of the nuclear family and its role in settler colonialism in the Americas, it's important to reiterate the relative historical "newness" of both the nuclear family and intimate terrorist relationships, as well as the origins of both in settler colonialism and the expansion of capitalism. Treatment of Black and Indigenous Peoples and women as objects to be bought and sold represented an emergence of the logic of capitalism in the new nation state. The nuclear family, dependent on women's legal subordination within the home through marriage, "after all, was the building block of the new social order in the conquered territories" (Hernández, 2017, p. 14). Tracing social patterns of coercive control and intimate terrorism brings us back to the invasion of colonial powers in the Americas. Kelly Lytle Hernandez, in her exploration of the origins of the carceral system in Los Angeles, points out that state violence through police and prison systems originated in the genocide of Indigenous Peoples in the Tongva Basin (2017). In other words, the tendency to treat others as objects to possess and control, which is so prevalent in high-risk family violence relationships, is a consequence of the expansion of capitalism through the installation of settler regimes in Indigenous territory. An intimate terrorist partner relies on the same practices of coercion and control to maintain order in the home that police forces used (and continue to use) to maintain order in the nation state.

Neil Websdale's research on family-killing demonstrates that the conditions experienced by those who kill their family emerge from modern-era emotional formations in response to social and political life. In *Familicidal Hearts*, Websdale explores 211 cases of familicide, defined as the "annihilation of the nuclear family as we have come to know it; a historical phenomenon of fairly recent origin and highly idiosyncratic emotional intensity" (2010, p. 7). The assertion that familicide is a recent historical development, tied to settler institutions, is important.

Drawing upon classical concepts of the sociological imagination, Websdale asserts that a familicidal heart is one that is "haunted by modern patterns and atmospheres of feeling" (2010, p. 13). The sociological imagination draws attention to the leaky and constantly evolving boundaries between our "selves" and our social world. It disrupts binary notions of nature/nurture and forces us to think through how we all negotiate our "selves" in relation to others. Websdale's notion of a familicidal heart, as a consequence of contemporary life in the modern settler state, is deeply relevant to the study of domestic homicide because his research demonstrates that familicide is a "consequence of modern era emotional life" (p. 1). This assertion counters carceral notions of violence as "natural" products of a few pathological individuals. Websdale situates family-killing in historical context by analyzing the relationship between family-killing and the "monopoly over the use of violence and the rights of taxation" (p. 13) used by emerging settler states to create the conditions for industrial capitalism.

When we work to understand the patterns of domestic homicide in historical context, it is important to note that the expansion of British colonial powers took place during a time when the emergence of industrial capitalism drastically shifted relationships between the individual, the market and their intimate relations: "By the late 1700s, people in Britain could legally enter into different kinds of contractual arrangements whereby they could own land, sell their labor, and possess their identities, all of which were formed through their relationship to capital and the state" (Moreton-Robinson, 2015, p. 113). If we understand possessiveness and coercion to be hallmarks of high-risk family violence that result in homicide, then we must look back to where cultural tendencies to claim ownership over others began. Websdale identifies how these shifts toward "modern landscapes of feeling," which arose during this time of social and political upheaval, coincided with the earliest recorded incidences of familicide: "The killing of the entire nuclear family unit—spouse, children, oftentimes followed by the suicide of the perpetrator—appears confined to modern times, or more precisely the period from 1755 in the United States" (p. 87). Thus, the emotional conditions experienced by those who resolve their feelings of dispossession, shame and distress through killing their loved ones are created by the social and political conditions of colonization. Patriarchy, in the Americas, is, and was, merely a consequence of this larger process of theft, dispossession, violence and coercive control by colonial regimes.

The carceral feminist approach, which relies on what Richie (2012) refers to as "overly simplistic analysis" (p. 2) that blames gender inequality as the sole cause of family violence, is only telling a small part of the story we need to understand in order to prevent domestic homicide and transform our conditions. If we apply feminist approaches of understanding violence in the "control context in which they are embedded" (Johnson, 2008), we must understand state violence in the ongoing control context of settler colonialism. When I acknowledge the well-researched and established features of a coercive control relationship and compare these features of high-risk intimate partner violence to a historical understanding of colonial violence in settler Canada, it is clear that intimate terrorism, as it outlined by Johnson (2008) and Stark (2009), is an intimate expression of state terrorism. Surveillance, legitimation, threat of punishment and strategic use of force are foundational elements of policing in settler-colonial states. Intimate terrorism can be understood as the application of state-sanctioned methods of policing within an intimate context through the use of coercive control relations. Turning our attention to the differing dynamics and effects of intimate partner violence allows us to identify when and where violent relations emerge as a state-building project in the lives of those who face dispossession or a loss of power in racial capitalism.

I must acknowledge that the continued assault of Black, Indigenous, poor and mentally ill people by police forces cannot be reduced to a single frame of analysis. Different communities face compound risks for police and intimate partner violence that must be understood contextually and historically. As Maynard reminds us, "the racial logic of slavery and settler colonialism take different forms and are not reducible to one another; anti-Blackness and settler colonialism rest on somewhat different foundations" (2017, p. 11). Drawing our attention to how coercive control dynamics characterize police violence allows us to distinguish between intimate partner abuse that is a situational reaction to stress or conflict or a potentially lethal reaction to dispossession and loss of power within racial capitalism.

## Possessiveness, Power and Strategic Violence

We know that the most dangerous type of abusive relationship involves intimate terrorism. We know that this type of abuse is characterized by coercion, threats of punitive violence, surveillance and a context of control over the autonomy and personhood of the survivor. This type of abuse sustains itself through processes of legitimation, whereby an abuser convinces the survivor that they have the authority or reason to engage in violence or punishment. Often, risk for domestic homicide is triggered by separation, something the abusive partner experiences as a total loss of control over their partner. Jacquelyn Campbell notes: "When the worst incident of abuse was triggered by the victim's having left the abuser for another partner or by the abuser's jealousy, there was a nearly 5-fold increase in femicide risk" (2003, p. 1091). Feelings of possessiveness and sexual jealousy in the treatment of a survivor as an "object" create a sense of entitlement. This sense of entitlement and aggrieved possessiveness allows a coercive partner to feel it is their authority to decide whether their partner lives or dies. Feminist critiques of the sexual objectification of women (MacKinnon, 1987; Dworkin, 1974) ring true when we interrogate the conditions that lead an abusive partner to kill; objectification and possessiveness facilitate violence. But where do these practices come from? Carceral feminist strategies that end their analysis with blaming the patriarchy effectively stop short of interrogating the role of white supremacy and colonialism in the imposition of patriarchy and sexual objectification in our shared history.

Mike Gouldhawke (2020) reminds us that police violence, since the founding of the Northwest Mounted Police Force in the early colonial period, has included repression of labour organizing and other forms of social protest throughout the twentieth century: "In 1919, during the Winnipeg General Strike, the RCMP opened fire on a crowd of workers, killing two and injuring dozens, helping to crush the strike and win greater significance for the force in the eyes of the capitalist ruling class." This can easily be applied in the context of intimate terrorism. Evan Stark writes: "The primary harm abusive men inflict is political, not physical, and reflects the deprivation of rights and resources that are critical to personhood and citizenship" (2009, p. 5). All coercive control, when it utilizes the same strategies taught and maintained through the ongoing project of colonial state-building, is political.

Police forces who use violence to quash labour protests or arrest Indigenous land defenders, and abusive partners who threaten and harm survivors who stand up for their rights or autonomy, are both participating in the ongoing colonial project of maintaining illegitimate rule of life and land that is not their own. It comes down to who feels the authority to coerce, attack or kill and who, historically and today, is usually the object of violence that is used to restore stability to a fragile or illegitimate ruler. We can no longer ignore the connections between what Stark (2009) and other feminist researchers on intimate partner violence have characterized as "high-risk intimate partner violence" and the violence that was used to conquer and control the Indigenous territories we now call home. Theft of land and the destruction of Indigenous sovereignty must be seen, today, in structures and processes of family violence that aspire to the values of white supremacy and heteropatriarchal family formations.

## Note

1. For more information on Kelly's story, see Carmen Ponciano, "Former officer's report aims to 'expose' police internal practice," *CBC News,* Jul 18, 2017. <https://www.cbc.ca/news/canada/kitchener-waterloo/kelly-donovan-waterloo-regional-police-former-constable-report-1.4210472> or her new book, *Police Line: Do Not Cross: Silencing a Canadian Police Whistleblower* <https://www.barnesandnoble.com/w/police-line-kelly-donovan/1137331302>.

# Portapique

It is April 2020. I am working on the third chapter for this book. We have been on COVID lockdown for just under a month.

I nervously flip between screens on my computer. On one, pages of black-and-white notes about intimate partner homicide, colonialism and prison abolition. On the other, a web screen with live news updates about an active shooter in a rural town not too far from where I live.

Earlier this morning we turned the dial on our old radio to pick up CBC Radio One and learned that police were pursuing an active shooter in Colchester County.

I rubbed my eyes and muttered to myself,

"Domestic homicide. He attacked his partner and now he's on a rampage. They are going to find her injured or dead somewhere once they catch him."

My partner nodded quietly as we listened to the news.

I remind myself not to jump to conclusions. I know, however, that the tragedy unfolding about a hundred kilometres from our home is one that began in the context of intimate partner violence. Friends and colleagues start messaging each other. We all know. We are waiting for the journalists to start calling around for expert commentary about intimate partner homicide. But none of us predicted the scale of this tragedy.

I wrap my hands around the warmth of a coffee cup and try not to think about it. Pulling my housecoat tightly around myself, I get up from my desk and take a seat on the floor to play with my daughter in the living room.

They find him a few hours later at a gas station, and he is shot by police. The same gas station where I fill up my station wagon on my morning commutes to campus.

I sit and write these words as police are slowly uncovering a landscape of torched homes, bodies riddled with bullet holes and a pathway of devastation and tragedy across Colchester County that will mark the largest mass shooting in Canadian history.[1]

I am going to call him the shooter. Journalists use his initials, GW.

Talking about the shooter feels terrible. It feels wrong.

Twenty-two lives were lost after what began as an argument with his common-law partner ended in a tragedy of unspeakable proportions.

Misogynistic culture often glorifies or excuses patriarchal violence. Misogynistic news coverage tends to memorialize killers. It sometimes paints them as victims and ignores the ones who lost their lives due to violence. Sometimes killers are motivated by the fame they think they'll win if they do something terrible. I recall the van attack in Toronto, where ten were killed and sixteen injured when an incel intentionally plowed his vehicle into a group of women. I think about other mass shooters who wanted their violence to serve as a cautionary tale to put women, Muslims, queer folks in their place. I think about the mosque shooting in Quebec City, where six were killed and five more injured when a white supremacist opened fire on worshippers. Marc Lépine. We remember his name. We remember that he shot fourteen women because he was angry about feminism. We don't always remember the names of his victims, even though we read them aloud each year on December 6 at memorials to commemorate them.

I think about the families who have to live in Colchester County, haunted by a trajectory of violence that travelled through six different communities and continues to echo on our screens, on the radio, on the evening news. It fucking reverberates here.

I need to talk about the shooter. I've known enough killers to know that no one kills like this in a vacuum. I have known enough survivors to know that preventing future killing is one of the only ways we can atone for the sins of a culture that breeds this kind of violence.

If we don't talk about what makes a killer, we'll never stop it.

I try to tell this story in a way that does not excuse violence. I believe in holding killers accountable. I don't believe that we need to empathize to understand. We can understand without feeling sorry for them. Pity and understanding are not the same thing.

Reasons and excuses are not the same thing. Drunk drivers get into accidents because they are drunk. That doesn't make it okay. Reasons are not excuses—but they can be important information if we take violence prevention and transformation seriously.

Survivors who are closest to a tragedy like this shouldn't have to do this work. The closer you are to ground zero of a tragedy, the further you should be from doing the abolitionist work of salvaging the human from the violence they perpetrated. No one should have to forgive the person who killed their loved one. I guess I don't follow the script about forgiveness as some kind of moral virtue.

Anger should follow its own path. Survivors are already working hard enough at their own healing.

As someone who is far from this tragedy in a personal sense, I see it as my job to do the hard work of understanding where the violence came from and how we can prevent it in the future.

⤲◇⤳

At the point that I am writing this, the RCMP is being forced to release partially redacted documents to a consortium of news media about the events that transpired on April 18 and 19, 2020.

Here is what is known so far:

On April 18, 2020, the shooter got into an argument with his common-law partner.

After he dragged her outside by her hair, shot at her and then handcuffed her inside one of his decommissioned cop cars, she manages to escape and hides in the woods under the roots of a tree.

Around 10 p.m., a 911 call is made by someone in Portapique.

When officers arrive half an hour later, they find bodies on the road and burning buildings. They learn that the shooter is driving what looks like a police cruiser.

Thirteen victims are found deceased.

They do not find the shooter. The RCMP sends out a tweet about the investigation but does not use the emergency alert system to alert neighbours or those who are not on Twitter.

The next morning, the shooter kills three more people.

His partner comes out of hiding in the woods and tells police that he is in possession of multiple firearms and is probably driving a replica RCMP cruiser.

The shooter continues to drive around, killing. He kills a woman on the side of the highway.

Using his RCMP uniform and cruiser, he pulls two separate vehicles over, killing both occupants. One of them was pregnant.

He encounters two police officers. He shoots one officer, who survives.

The second officer, Constable Heidi Stevenson, is killed as she rams his vehicle head-on, trying to stop him.

The shooter then kills a bystander who stops to help after seeing the police vehicles engulfed in flames. He kills another woman in her home.

He is eventually shot by police at the Enfield Big Stop gas station.

꙳◈꙳

A few weeks after the shootings, a former neighbour told the media that she had reported domestic violence and the shooter's cache of weapons to the RCMP in 2013. Brenda, the neighbour, recounts a story of the shooter's partner running to her home for help. Brenda tells the media that she was terrified of the shooter and afraid he would retaliate if he knew that his partner had run to her home for assistance.

Brenda is a veteran and retired member of the Canadian Armed Forces. She knew about the domestic violence in the home for years before the mass shooting happened. There were other witnesses. Her husband had seen the shooter's illegal guns. Witnesses had seen the shooter strangling his partner.

When Brenda finally told her story to the RCMP in 2013 they did not charge him. She recounts how the shooter became aggressive after she spoke with the RCMP. He would drive slowly around their house and sit parked outside.

Brenda eventually left the area with her husband. She said they were afraid of the shooter and wanted to be far away from him.

≈◇≈

There are reports that the shooter used to park in front of his partner's car so she couldn't escape or leave the rural area where they lived.

Domestic violence advocates chime in with suggestions for "coercive control" laws. They explain that this kind of behaviour points to coercive control or intimate terrorism.

Despite my abolitionist politics, I remember being excited about coercive control laws when they first appeared in the United Kingdom. I also remember reading about how impossible they are to use in practice. They don't work. Police are hesitant to use them, the laws are difficult to apply, and survivors are hesitant to accept any police involvement.

We have pro-arrest policies in Nova Scotia. This means that if there is evidence of domestic violence, then police are required to lay a charge regardless of whether the victim cooperates. Those laws were not used either in this case. It appears that they didn't even investigate the firearms complaint.

The shooter did not have a gun licence.

Strangling is an indicator of a high-risk for domestic homicide. So is access to firearms.

Throw an impending separation and occupational stress into the equation, and we have a statistical likelihood for homicide.

I feel nauseous thinking about all the red flags that were known about and not acted on. I feel nauseous thinking about how many people in his life lived in fear of his violence and instability.

Brenda, a sixty-two-year-old veteran, was forced to leave her community because she tried to help a victim of intimate partner violence.

≈◇≈

Information begins to trickle in about the shooter's habits before the shootings began.

Media reports claim that the shooter was a "survivalist" and was convinced the pandemic would ruin him. Despite amassing many properties, including income properties, and running a successful denturist business, he was convinced the pandemic would create chaos and that he would lose everything. He armed himself to the teeth to protect himself for "when the money runs out." He appeared intent on defending himself and his property against some kind of occupational or existential threat.

There are multiple stories about dubious and fraudulent business practices, specifically about how the shooter acquired properties. In one case, a man reports that the shooter tricked him into signing over his home after the shooter provided a short-term loan to the homeowner. In another case, the shooter's uncle reveals that his property was stolen after accepting short-term bridge financing from the shooter.

One of the victims in Portapique lived in a property that was the subject of a legal dispute between the shooter and his uncle. There are reports that he swindled someone out of their shares in an apartment building, jointly owned with his friend, Tom Evans. He is described as a bully who acquired multiple properties through fraudulent and unethical means and who used brute force and threats to impose his will on those around him.

He was also obsessed with the RCMP. The shooter spent years amassing RCMP paraphernalia. He told his neighbours that his meticulously restored RCMP replica cruiser was a tribute to fallen officers.

Reports surface that there was a police bulletin about him years ago, after someone reported that he wanted to kill cops.

It was no secret that he had a replica cruiser. I even drove by it a few times, parked outside his denture clinic in Dartmouth the summer before the tragedy.

I think about how the earliest incarnation of the RCMP helped legitimate the fraudulent theft of land from Métis, Cree, Anishinaabe, Dene and Nakota Nations to the Hudson's Bay Company.

The first federal police were agents for colonizers who sought to expropriate and exploit Indigenous territories for continued expansion of the Dominion of Canada. I think about the myth of the benevolent Mountie as the "defender of the North." I think about how bullying, coercion and theft of land were the foundational practices of Canadian statehood.

I think about my friend Kelly, a survivor who became a cop to help end gender-based violence and now needs a security detail because she blew the whistle on police corruption. I think about the bravery and courage of Constable Heidi Stevenson as she rammed the shooter's vehicle before he shot her. I choke up thinking about her family, her children.

I think about all the reports of sexual harassment and misogyny in the RCMP.

They make a big deal out of Constable Stevenson's funeral. I hope and pray that her experience in policing was better than Kelly's was.

My friend El is a journalist and an activist. She is a Black feminist with a mind like a fucking diamond. She posts about how the memorialization of the death of an officer works to conceal how the RCMP may have mishandled this incident and how the shooter's fetish for police should caution us all against turning the tragedy into a depoliticized memorial for fallen officers. She is mercilessly attacked online. She is told that "this is not the time" and called insensitive for bringing these issues up while people are grieving.

Police are heroes. Full stop.

The Snowbirds, military fighter jets, fly over Nova Scotia to cheer us up. Pomp and pageantry. The jets crisscross the sky. The province salutes them in response. This is it: our collective funeral. A military airshow. Everyone is emotional.

The irony of using military fighter jets to cheer us up after a killing spree by a police- and weapons-obsessed shooter is palpable.

Then the RCMP announce that the shooter's surviving partner is going to be charged because she helped supply him with ammunition. The shooter, himself, was never charged. Not when he beat her in front of neighbours. Not when he killed twenty-two people and then himself.

A consortium of media outlets continues to fight for the release of more unredacted documents from the RCMP about the tragedy.

Information about the shooter's childhood reveals experiences of severe abuse at the hands of his father. The shooter's uncle tells a story about his father choking his mother. The shooter's father is described as "manipulative, possessive and violent."

A family friend claims that the shooter's father forced his then nine-year-old son to shoot and kill his dog as punishment for not cleaning up after it. The same interview recounts the shooter, at age five, being forced to watch his father burn his security blanket that he had since he was a baby because he was too attached to it. His uncle tells journalists that he tried to take the shooter from his parents as a toddler because he did not want him to grow up in such a violent home.

Another story reveals how the shooter had a brother who was given up for adoption. The person interviewed for the story says they believe the shooter snapped when he found out that he had a brother who was given away to a loving home. It is surmised that the shooter could not fathom how or why his mother would let his brother be raised in a good home while he was forced to endure the abuse he grew up with.

Journalists trace four generations of humiliation, threats and violent abuse in the shooter's family.

It strikes me that they don't talk about how many rural towns have no community-based programs for family violence. There are few public or affordable men's mental health services.[2]

We don't talk enough about how every killer was once a child who probably needed our help. I tweet a long thread about how community-based family violence programs and youth-serving programs that help young survivors of family violence might be one way we could help heal from this tragedy.

I feel like I'm screaming into the void.

I receive an email from a former correctional officer who knew one of the victims. He tells me he is a victim of childhood sexual abuse. He tells me he became a correctional officer because he wanted to feel powerful and safe. He wanted to wear a uniform and be in charge. He didn't want anyone to hurt him again. He tells me he thinks a lot of men who experienced childhood abuse aspire to be powerful—to be the kind of people who could have saved them from the abuse they suffered as children. He breaks my heart.

I think about the how the shooter's uncle was an RCMP officer.

⇝ ◊ ⇜

I got a message from a journalist after speaking publicly on social media about a need for youth-support programs and better rural mental health options for survivors of family violence.

He wants to talk on the phone.

He asks me what I know about killers. I talk to him for a bit about the research I did for this book and summarize Websdale's book on "familicidal hearts" and typologies of intimate partner violence. I talk at length about some of the men I worked with in prison.

He tells me about some interviews he has done about the Portapique shooting. He has information he is not ready to publish; he tells me he is not sure that he should or can publish it. He tells me about a man named Tom Evans in New Brunswick.[3] Tom is an infamous bully and disgraced lawyer with ties to organized crime. He lost his licence to practise law after being charged with sexually assaulting a young man.

This man, Tom Evans, was reportedly the shooter's best friend. Despite what is almost a twenty-year age difference between them, this journalist tells me that he wonders if the shooter was groomed into an abusive relationship with him. He tells me that Evans would groom young men and then convince them to sexually assault other young men as retaliation for perceived slights. He's heard this in multiple interviews.

I tell him that it is common for survivors of family violence to be groomed or exploited by predators like this. It feels awful to speak of the shooter as a victim. It feels awful to think about the layers of pain that led up to the tragedy.

The man on the other end of the line is sick with this information. He has interviewed surviving family members and witnesses. He has been knee-deep in the trauma and the pain and been vicariously processing the tragedy.

A month or so later there are reports in the media about Tom Evans and his relationship with the shooter. It's revealed that Evans had been convicted for various crimes, including supplying alcohol to minors, shooting 197 rounds of ammunition at a crowded youth camp, tax evasion and helping members of a drug cartel try to break their members out of prison.

One article mentions that Tom Evans was "like a father" to the shooter.

❧ ◊ ❧

I can't stop thinking about the fucking Snowbirds and their toxic jet fuel and pageantry. How did coercion and control become both the problem and the solution here? Glorification of state triumph through military conquest shouldn't be the answer to resolving feelings of pain, dispossession and misery.

The snake is eating its tail while we salute the sky.

## Notes

1. Public Safety Canada, Nova Scotia Shooting Incident – Timeline, April 27, 2020. <https://www.publicsafety.gc.ca/cnt/trnsprnc/brfng-mtrls/prlmntry-bndrs/20200730/021/index-en.aspx>.
2. For an excellent look at the importance of children's mental health care and homicide prevention in the context of Portapique, check out Sarah Ritchie's podcast *13 Hours*, Episode 13: "How ending child abuse and improving mental health care could prevent mass shootings," *Global News*. <https://globalnews.ca/news/7750967/ending-child-abuse-mental-health-preventing-mass-shootings/>.
3. For more information on the shooter's relations with a sexual predator and participation in land theft, see Stephen Maher, "The Nova Scotia killer's dark past, and a mysterious $300,000," Maclean's, October 16, 2020. <https://www.macleans.ca/news/canada/the-nova-scotia-killers-dark-past-and-a-mysterious-300000/>.

# Occupation, Racial Capitalism and the "Familicidal Heart"

Occupation: the principal business of one's life
- the possession, use or settlement of land
- the holding and control of an area by military force.
                                    — Merriam Webster Dictionary

"Perhaps the greatest contribution to primary prevention would be to develop an understanding of why people use violence and what might make them stop."
                                    — Leigh Goodmark, 2018, loc. 2752

"The value of work, along with its centrality to our lives, is one of the most stubbornly naturalized and apparently self-evident elements of modern and late, or postmodern, capitalist societies."
                                    — Kathi Weeks, 2011, loc. 816

Supreme Court of Nova Scotia. April 2, 2018. I'm at Butcher's trial.

Judge Joshua Arnold is presiding over jury selection in the trial of Nicholas Butcher for the killing of Kristin Johnston.
The first woman is nervous. She doesn't know where to put her purse.

"Nicholas Butcher, a graduate of Dalhousie law school..."

The judge lists Nick's occupation every time he asks a potential juror if they have formed too much of an opinion from media accounts of the murder to be an impartial juror. It feels like I've heard "graduate of Dalhousie law school" at least a dozen times this morning.

"Kristin Johnston, a yoga instructor..."

She owned her yoga studio. She was a small business owner. I don't understand why occupational details are included every time the victim and accused are mentioned.

Judge Arnold addresses Butcher's lawyers. He wants to know if Planetta — Butcher's lawyer — has questions about the occupation of potential jurors.

Planetta wants to know.

The occupation of each juror is now a matter of record. Data analyst. Army reservist. Occupation unknown. Electrical engineer...

In a previous chapter, I discussed the historical emergence of "coercive control" in colonial state policies strategically enacted to subdue, control and maintain illegitimate claim to Indigenous territory. Coercive control relations, the type of abusive relationship that poses the highest risk for domestic homicide, are underpinned by a "possessive logic" whereby the abusive partner engages in a wide range of tactics to maintain control over their partner, seeking to "possess" them in every sense of the word. This possessive logic (Moreton-Robinson, 2015) is central to the expansion of settler colonialism, which relies on white supremacy to justify and legitimate theft of land, resources and bodies from Indigenous Peoples and the transatlantic slave trade. This normative practice of coercive control in public and private life can be tragic when it combines with occupational stress and childhood experiences with neglect or violence.

For the alienated and dispossessed, what is work, if not coercion? In a financialized market, where most of us lack the means to survive—to eat, find shelter or care for our kin—without exchanging our labour for cash, we can't choose whether we work or not. Without choice, how can we consent? Bob Black (2009) wrote: "Work is production enforced by economic or political means, by the carrot or the stick. (The carrot is just the stick by other means)." Our capitalist system, facilitated by the expansion of colonial extraction and industrialization, was enacted through practices of objectification and dehumanization that used racism as an excuse for the continued theft of land and labour from Black and other racialized peoples. In *Black Marxism* (2000), Cedric Robinson argues that capitalism and racism must be understood together. Racial capitalism, he argues, is a system whereby capital maintains a system of unfettered growth and expansion through exploitive extraction of value from racialized peoples. In this sense, capitalism cannot exist without white supremacist logics, which legitimate the tremendous inequalities and injustices that are perpetuated in the labour market.

One of the major risk factors for domestic homicide is occupational stress or unemployment. I previously explored how early colonial policies were intended to nurture consumer desire in the settler class to secure their participation in the workforce and generate surplus wealth for the Empire. In this chapter I explore another, perhaps unintended, effect of nurturing a desire for "objects" and possessions and its role in catalyzing homicidal violence. In the following section, I describe the ways in which occupational stress in racial capitalism creates existential insecurity that can trigger domestic homicide. Attention to the subjectivities produced under conditions of occupation reveal the emotional conditions of domestic homicide. These occupying forces, coupled with heteropatriarchal notions of masculinity, shape the internal contours of a familicidal heart (Websdale, 2010) and, when blended with feelings of humiliation, shame and powerlessness, become a toxic cocktail in which domestic terrorists turn to homicide to resolve feelings of shame and failure. The intimate terrorist (Johnson, 2008; Stark, 2009) is one where the self has collapsed into the occupying forces of racial capitalism. It is clear that, for some killers, their failure as a worker is experienced as a deep existential threat. If we acknowledge that the intimate terrorist has no subjective vitality outside of the forces and demands of the market, then perhaps greater attention to work *as coercion* and a refusal of the conditions of work in racial capitalism might open possibilities for a safer future for survivors of family violence. In a general sense, we must consider our relations with "work" as a form of coercion that normalizes coercive control in everyday life.

We can't blame everything on trauma. Forensic psychiatry tells us little about socio-historical origins of domestic homicide. The field of forensic mental health relies on carceral conceptions of a criminal as a social anomaly, one whose personal life history, family origins and patterns of behaviour can shed light on particular pathological transgressions. Much of the research into perpetrator characteristics, family history and risk factors focuses on the individual experiences of the perpetrator rather than on their relations with social structures and processes that drive their internalized emotional experiences.

Forensic psychiatry can, however, offer a window into some of the emotional or psychological patterns associated with domestic killers. Although they fall short on connecting the dots between the structures and processes of colonialism, racial capitalism and domestic terrorism, these patterns offer us a series of sketches or impressions that can reveal how a dangerous convergence of toxic masculine expectations, occupational failure and overwhelming feelings of shame and humiliation can result in domestic homicide. Various studies (Kivisto, 2015; Johnson and Ferraro, 2000) show that experiences of childhood abuse or the presence of intimate partner abuse in the family home impacted a substantial *minority* of men who perpetrate domestic homicide, with only approximately one-quarter of incarcerated perpetrators of domestic homicide having experienced violence in their family of origin. In one study, it was demonstrated that "80 percent of the men whose parents had been severely violent do not grow up to be wife beaters" (Johnson, 2008, p. 34). Although Johnson and others point out that coercive control relationships do have a higher rate of childhood trauma than other types of violent relationship, it is not the sole cause of domestic homicide.

Other factors, such as access to firearms, strong adherence to heteropatriarchal gender norms, occupational stress and a history of coercive and controlling behaviour in the relationship are more strongly associated with domestic homicide (Campbell et al., 2003). Patriarchal possessiveness, again, weighs heavily in domestic homicides. "Enmeshment" is a term used by psychiatrists to describe the collapse of a perpetrator's identity and self-worth into their ability to control their partners and children. A killer's status in the social world can be mediated and maintained by the ways in which they negotiate their status inside their domestic spaces. A possessive, or enmeshed, killer views "their family members as possessions that they control or [they] don't see any boundaries between their identity, their wife and their children" (Gelles, cited in Auchter, 2010, p. 10). In other words, the killer sees their kin as objects who are extensions of their self-worth and identity. However, another form of enmeshment that goes unrecognized in our attempts to prevent homicide is the enmeshment of a person's identity and value with their occupational identity. For cisgender men in European colonial cultures, their "occupation" colonizes their entire sense of self. Their value to community is often understood as their value in the labour market. During times of economic recession, unemployment or occupational stress, this can have devastating impacts. Nicholas Butcher, the Portapique shooter and Lionel Desmond (who I discuss later) all experienced devastating occupational or financial stress in the period leading up to the killings.

## Occupation and Domestic Homicide

Numerous studies demonstrate an increased risk for intimate partner violence and homicide during times of occupational stress, such as sudden job loss or financial hardship from changes in the global market (Schneider et al., 2016; Benson and Fox, 2002). Michael Benson and Greer Fox (2002) found that periods of unemployment, as well as employment in jobs that included significant overtime and workplace stress, were both predictors of increased violence. Campbell et al. (2003) provide comprehensive data toward the creation of "domestic homicide risk assessment checklists," and their work demonstrates that unemployment represents one of the most dramatic risk factors for intimate partner homicide:

> In comparing our femicide perpetrators with other abusive men, we found that unemployment was the most important demographic risk factor for acts of intimate partner femicide. In fact, abusers' lack of employment was the only demographic risk factor that significantly predicted femicide risks after we controlled for a comprehensive list of more proximate risk factors, increasing risks 4-fold relative to the case of employed abusers.

Homicide risk assessment is often part of an inter-agency approach embedded within carceral systems, which rely on police or victim services workers to go through the checklist with survivors once their partner has been charged with a crime to determine their risk for being killed. However, as Websdale points out, risk assessment practices represent "a denial of complex personhood and a profound misunderstanding of the continuities and complexities of figurations of feelings, familial atmospheres of feeling, and emotional styles" (2010, p. 276). In other words, risk assessment practices that are currently deployed through carceral approaches to family violence often miss the whole story when we are trying to understand the conditions that make someone kill. Unemployment is strongly associated with domestic homicide, but not all unemployed men represent a threat to the lives of their partners. If we shift our focus from trying to predict domestic

homicide at the individual level to understanding our socio-historical genealogy of family and partner killing, it allows us to see the cultural origins of
domestic homicide, thus providing a framework for transformative justice
that is specific to homicide.

Another notable risk factor for men's violence is adherence to heteropatriarchal gender norms. Feminist literature on intimate partner violence has
a long history of tracing the relationship between masculine expectations
for dominance, aggression and power and men's use of violence in their
intimate lives. A recent report (The Men's Project and Michael Flood,
2020) from Australia demonstrate that men's adherence to heteropatriarchal gender norms is:

- 25 times more accurate than a range of demographic variables in
  predicting the use of physical violence, sexual harassment, verbal bullying and cyber bullying;
- 22 times more accurate in predicting the experience of physical violence, verbal bullying and cyber bullying;
- 11 times more accurate than demographics at predicting very risky
  drinking; and
- 10 times more accurate than demographics at predicting negative
  feelings and emotions.

Embedded within these heteropatriarchal norms is the core of what
makes men turn to violence during times of occupational stress. Toxic
masculine expectations position men's role as "breadwinner," where their
income stands in as their quantified value as a human. David Frayne (2015)
argues that work colonizes every moment of our life in Western capitalist
democracies. Echoing Merivale's treatise on the importance of nurturing
consumer desire as a means to secure labour participation, Frayne argues
that contemporary subjects often use work to mask or escape from the pain
of insecurity in neoliberal democracies that are void of community and
social safety nets, where the "world of consumer goods, with its escapes,
luxuries and distractions promises to fill the existential void (or at least to
help us forget about it for a while)" (2015, p. 179). Six generations after
Professor Merivale's lecture about the need to nurture abstract desire for
wealth and denial of pleasure to secure settler participation in generating
surplus wealth for the Empire, the effects of his policies continue to ring
clear.

ॐ ◇ ॐ

*The following section details a conversation I had with someone convicted of sexual and family violence and includes some of their thoughts on rehabilitation and social change. Please don't hesitate to skip this section if you just can't or don't want to dig into what a rapist has to say about these things.*

I am sitting in a church basement, having a conversation with a formerly incarcerated person who was convicted of family and sexual violence. We are talking about a program he has been involved in since his release. He attributes this program with his newfound perspective on his harmful behaviour.

He has been in counselling in addition to participating in a program that brings sexual offenders together, at various stages of their rehabilitation, to provide guidance for each other and to hold each other accountable to addressing their harms and learning new ways of being in relation to others.

Our conversation turns to this manuscript. I tell him I am working on a book about domestic homicide. He tells me he doesn't know much about homicide, but he does know about family violence and sexual assault.

I ask him what kind of changes we can make as a society to help reduce family violence. We talk for a while about a need for community-based counselling and support for youth. Then he is quiet. He tells me that, as a society, we focus entirely too much on "what we do" rather than who we are or what our values are.

He recounts stories about how, when he was actively harming his family, he was a proud man. He did well at work, he was a soccer coach, and he was held in high regard at his church and in his community. Every time he met someone new, the question was "what do you do?"

He tells me how, because of experiences with neglect in his childhood, he developed an unhealthy obsession with desperately trying to "do" anything he could to make people love him. This led to some very pathological behaviour.

I agree. Our commonly accepted first question in social exchange conflates our occupation with our selves, as if what we do for work gives the most important information about us.

He tells me he never really learned to live according to his own values. Everything he ever did was to get approval from others. He says, looking back, he recognizes how pathetic it was. How even when he ordered lunch at a restaurant with his family, he felt anxious about what to order and would often copy the order of someone else at the table. He was perpetually insecure.

Sexual violence was a pathological attempt to resolve his feelings of insecurity.

We talk about his childhood. The short version is that he lost his parents when he was young and was raised by distant family who were not that interested in raising him—or being his family. He says they felt obligated to raise him, but he couldn't really think of anyone who loved him after his parents died.

He talks about how, every time he was asked "what do you do?" by another adult, he felt pathetic and small. He would think about the sexual assaults he had perpetrated. He would think about how he manipulated his family. He would think about how he didn't make enough money at his job.

He says he learned in prison that the biggest barrier to changing his own behaviour was overcoming shame so he could think clearly about what actually caused him to do such terrible things. He says the shame clouded everything, and when he felt ashamed of himself, this is what often drove the violent behaviour. He says that when he was able to see beyond the shame and feelings of self-loathing he had felt his whole life, he realized what he really believed in, and that has been the guiding light to changing his behaviour.

Shame and self-loathing about what he had done got in the way of him doing the personal work of becoming a safer person who doesn't exploit or assault others.

I tell him that I am surprised by his answer. I tell him that I was expecting him to say that he learned to objectify or treat women poorly. He agrees that this kind of misogyny is terrible and admits he made misogynistic jokes in the past. But he says that the worst thing for making him abusive was not what he was taught about women, but what he was taught about being a man.

Determining your values and beliefs is an important part of the rehabilitative program he now volunteers for. He says he thinks when we meet someone new, we should ask them what they believe in. He figures that's a better judge of character. And it would help us act more in line with what we think is right.

If you can't do what you believe in, then something's gotta change, right?

## Emotionally Dependent verus Antisocial Killers

In feminist and forensic psychiatric literature about domestic homicide, researchers identify two main types of killer. Some refer to the "under-controlled, dysregulated" killer, whose antisocial behaviour and outward displays of anger give an indication of their capacity for violence, or the "over-controlled, dysregulated killer," who deeply represses feelings of rage, shame and resentment and works hard to appear well-adjusted and harmless (Kivisto, 2015). Similarly, in Websdale's study of familicide, he observed that most killers possess either a "civil reputable heart" or a "livid coercive" one. Johnson (2008) also identifies two types of intimate terrorist:

> Antisocial intimate terrorists are sociopathic personalities who are willing to use violence to have their way in many situations, not just with their partner. Emotionally dependent intimate terrorists are not generally violent, but feel that they must take complete control over their partner in order not to lose her. (2008, p. 31)

These distinctions between killers who outwardly display violence or anger and those who deeply suppress feelings of rage and shame have implications for how we understand both treatment and prevention.

Butcher is an over-controlled, dysregulated person. Perhaps, one with a civil reputable heart.

The emotionally dependent killer with a civil reputable heart is one who is less likely to have a prior history of violence, even though they may engage in coercive control. Behaviours such as stalking, repeated phone calls, tracking the movements of their partner through technological means and using threats of suicide to manipulate a partner into forgiving them or staying in the relationship may appear less harmful than the behaviour of a coercive control partner with a history of physical violence or expressing their rage in front of others. However, Donald Dutton and Greg Kerry assert that "suppressed rage, rather than expressed violence, may be more indicative of subsequent spousal homicide" (1999, p. 298). In other words, the abusive partner who may be *more* likely to commit domestic homicide may be the one who appears harmless, or even helpless, to a close bystander or family member.

Emotionally dependent abusers pose a challenge to carceral approaches to domestic homicide, which require evidence of an assault to intervene. They, much like Nicholas Butcher, can appear harmless and vulnerable to those who know them. "Neediness" and threats of suicide may indicate feelings of powerlessness, yet, despite their inner feelings of insecurity, these behaviours are not harmless and can result in tragic outcomes. Those in their inner circles may feel sorry for them, or they may chastise or critique a survivor for trying to leave their emotionally dependent and needy partner when they are in crisis. This "incipient emotional terrorism" (Johnson, 2008), or "non-violent coercive control," can mask the danger that exists in this kind of abuse (Crossman et al., 2016). Although it is unclear how many relationships characterized by non-violent coercive control end in homicide, there are implications to how we think through pathways to safety for those who live with an "incipient terrorist."

Stereotypes of a domestic abuser portray an outwardly angry, bullying man who exudes rage and volatility. Because emotionally dependent or needy partners don't appear as a credible threat to their partners, police may abstain from charging, or friends and family of the survivor might downplay or dismiss any fears the survivor may have. Stalking behaviours become minimized when an abusive partner seems powerless or pathetic to their peers, who often fail to hold them accountable for the ways in which stalking or surveillance is harmful. This type of abuser presents challenges for intervention, where those with little experience working with abusive people may not be able to distinguish an emotionally dependent incipient terrorist from someone who is simply depressed or down on their luck and needs peer support to get back on their feet. During times of occupational stress, the dangers posed by over-controlled emotional dysregulation or manipulative neediness are clear. For example, veiled threats of suicide to keep a partner in the relationship can signify coercive control. In times of occupational stress, a toxic cocktail of material dispossession (from job loss or financial hardship), a desire to regain self-worth by controlling the objects of their desire and internal feelings of misery or shame from poor self-confidence or childhood abuse can spark homicide as the coercive partner attempts to resolve these painful feelings.

## Cops and Soldiers: Non-Civilian, Reputable Hearts?

Militarized occupations that involve state-sanctioned violence present an increased risk for perpetrating violence outside of the job, too. Police and military personnel are more likely to engage in family violence (Macquarrie et al., in Jaffe et al., 2020). Domestic and international security forces are "male-dominated professions infused with strong patriarchal values" (p. 187), where, in both occupations, "controlled aggression may be required to deal with life-threatening events that also become a source of trauma" (Macquarrie et al., in Jaffe et al., 2020, p. 187). Although trauma, on its own, might not increase a risk for someone using violence in the home, coupled with a highly heteropatriarchal institutional culture that teaches forms of coercion or violence as necessary skills for the job, the likelihood of this violence increases significantly. Data shows that the Canadian military nurtures a culture of misogyny and sexual violence (Connolly, 2021). Research on perpetration of domestic violence by police points to a connection between cultures and attitudes in policing and attitudes that sanction coercion and use of force within the home:

> Perhaps one of the most complex associations between DV [domestic violence] and the role of a police officer is related to their regular use of coercive force and control over people. Police are trained in interrogation techniques and the appropriate use of power and coercive force. They are sometimes required to use physical force to maintain compliance. (Macquarrie et al., in Jaffe et al., 2020, p. 191)

Military and police institutions rely on coercion, with weapons or threats of punishment, to achieve their political ends. Police and military personnel also have access to firearms, which is another significant risk factor in the perpetration of domestic homicide (Campbell et al., 2003). In the following chapter, I reflect on the Desmond tragedy in Nova Scotia, where a former Canadian soldier killed his mother, estranged wife and daughter before taking his own life. During the Desmond Fatality Inquiry, a psychologist from the Occupational Stress Injury Clinic, which handles referrals for treatment from Veterans Affairs Canada, the Department of National

Defence and the RCMP, testified about his treatment of the killer. Although the killer's family members had repeatedly told media that the soldier was denied treatment for his PTSD and post-concussion syndrome (Bousquet, 2017), the psychologist told the inquiry that the soldier was referred to a six-month residential treatment program so that he could get support for his occupational stress injury twenty-four hours a day. However, "he left the program three months early and returned home" rather than continue treatment for occupationally acquired PTSD (Canadian Press, 2021). Despite confiding in clinical staff at the Occupational Stress Injury Clinic that he was undergoing marital stress and conflict within his relationship, there was no formalized process to assess his risks for domestic violence or homicide.

Occupational stress is a well-known risk factor for domestic homicide, but few occupational therapists or clinical staff in stress injury clinics receive training on identifying red flags for family violence. Furthermore, police and military are often depicted as heroes or benevolent protectors of our communities. This can contribute to how and why health care and legal agencies might miss the red flags associated with intimate partner violence in connection with police and military personnel. Where police and military personnel are upheld as symbols of heteropatriarchal valour, it also explains why some killers, such as the Portapique shooter and Marc Lépine, have an obsession with the military and police.

What makes someone kill?

In the preceding sections, I sketched out a complex constellation of factors that contribute to domestic homicide. Although, in each case, there are specific factors—either intersectional or unique to the person or family unit—that require careful attention and analysis, there are patterns and trends in what we know to be risk factors, or red flags, that precede a homicide.

Trauma on its own cannot be used as a generalized explanation for domestic homicide. We must acknowledge that trauma, or childhood neglect, combined with a strong commitment to heteropatriarchal values can create conditions where a killer sees homicide as the only resolution for feelings of powerlessness, threats of dispossession (financial or occupational) or shame for not meeting expectations for productivity and status. Coercive partners or parents kill when they are in severe crisis. The depths of their emotional or psychological crisis may not be apparent to those who are close to them, or, in many cases, their apparent distress may be interpreted as a cry for help at the expense of attention to their boundary-crossing or abusive behaviour. Carceral thinking forces us to see someone as either a victim or perpetrator (Russo, 2018). This kind of thinking makes it difficult to negotiate how we hold our kin accountable when they are in distress. When someone we love is suicidal, it is difficult to see how they may be abusive or to know when or how to step in when we feel they may harm someone else.

An abolitionist approach to forensic mental health studies would provide a better approach to accounting for someone's capacity to harm when they are in crisis. An abolitionist approach acknowledges that we all have the capacity to harm and that those who harm deserve care and justice, while still holding them (and ourselves) accountable for complicity in violence. An abolitionist perspective on occupational stress or crisis at the prospect of financial ruin, might envision intersections between movements for labour justice and advocacy for community-based mental health programs. Untangling ourselves, however, from the forces of occupation that render us vulnerable to existential insecurity at the prospect of financial ruin is no easy task. It requires careful analysis and movement-building against the colonization of our subjectivities from the ever-expanding forces of the market. It also requires that we disarm and defund police and military personnel, whose collective impunity from the consequences of coercive violence in public and private life perpetuates the cycle of violence.

## The Intimate Knowledge of Survivors

Survivors often know more about the causes of coercive abuse than clinicians, frontline workers or domestic violence "experts." Another argument for greater abolitionist attention to forensic psychiatry in the study of domestic homicide is that survivors are already familiar with the pain and distress experienced by their abusive partners. When we ignore the misery experienced by killers leading up to and during extreme acts of violence, we miss the ways in which survivors feel forced to enable or excuse abuse because they love their abusers and see that they are suffering. We leave survivors feeling alone in their intimate knowledge about their partner's misery. When we abandon abusive partners and don't name or acknowledge the causes of their pain, we leave survivors alone to plug the holes in the dam of their partner's misery, which works to enable, rather than stop, abuse.

After years of working in a victim services unit and implementing a high-risk case protocol for women who are identified as at high risk for intimate partner homicide, Verona Singer conducted a research project to determine whether survivors felt that the high-risk protocols were helpful or harmful to survivors. Singer argues that the dominant discourse in approaches to working with survivors of family violence is a carceral approach that views the abuser as unrepentant and powerful, the victim as helpless and the criminal justice system as the solution to punishing violence. She points out that this mainstream approach "assumes the only reasonable response to abuse is for the woman to leave the relationship" (2012, p. 120) and that programs for abusers are viewed with suspicion because "they would use up resources better directed at women and because such an approach inappropriately individualizes the problem and may be used to excuse men or diminish their responsibility" (p. 121). This "dogmatic and dichotomous" (p. 121) mindset works to alienate survivors, who have intimate and holistic knowledge about why their partner is abusive.

In interviews with survivors of high-risk family violence, Singer acknowledged that abusers were, without question, "brutal, narcissistic and frightening" (p. 123), yet survivors of their violence expressed that what they wanted and needed was community support for their abusive partner in addition to support for themselves and their children. Singer writes:

> I was most struck by the persistence with which the abused women emphasized the need for programs for their abusive partners. This reveals the tension between essentializing the abuser as always bad or as someone who needs help. Since I did not ask the women about their loving moments with the abuser there may be less in my findings to indicate the characterization of the men as troubled rather than evil, but the frequent reference by the women of the need for treatment programs (discussed more fully below) may suggest that at least some of the women saw some redeeming qualities in some of the men. (pp. 125–26)

It is easy to forget that even the most dangerous abusive partners, the intimate terrorists who present the greatest danger to the survival of our kin, are also human. It is easy to forget that even those who are harmed the most deeply see value in the lives of their kin who have abused them. Singer's work demonstrates that many survivors of high-risk family violence want and need us to help their abusive partners in holistic, rather than carceral, ways. Cary Ryan's research (2021) also demonstrates that survivors feel harmed by carceral approaches to punishing their partners to the exclusion of providing rehabilitative or mental health resources.

Reflecting on Maynard's assertion that we must resist the temptation of disposability in our abolitionist work with those who have harmed (2017), it is clear that we need to build movements for accountability for the most dangerous abusive partners long before they experience catastrophic or homicidal distress. If we don't intervene before a perfect storm of occupational stress, access to firearms and impending loss of a partner or family through the devolution of the relationship, we find ourselves in a situation where intervention could lead to tragedy. One area in which we can build movements for preventative healing is that of labour justice and labour organizing.

## Abolish Occupation?

If our toxic relations with "work" contribute to conditions that foster homicidal violence, then labour organizing and movements for justice for those who are unemployed or facing financial hardship can be one avenue to build healing projects before a tragedy occurs. Websdale urges us to see experiences of shame and humiliation as "socially and historically situated phenomena, not as intrapsychic manifestations of insecurity or low self-esteem" (2010, p. 273). We must build movements that not only respond to suicidality and depression but question the mechanisms that cause shame, rage and depression when we face unemployment or financial hardship.

Shame and humiliation arise from the relation of a subject to their social world. In settler colonial Canada and the United States, a Protestant work ethic, characteristic of British colonial cultures, attributes moral value to the misery of labour. European colonial cultures fetishize the hardship of "work." Frayne points out that unemployment is continually positioned as a failure of the individual, whereby "it is still maintained that were a person to present themselves a little better, put a little more effort in, or just believe in themselves, he or she could find work and climb out of poverty" (2015, p. 100). These "cultural" explanations, as he calls them, work to conceal the damaging impacts of a capitalist system that causes misery for most and profit for few. He writes: "Perhaps the biggest crime of these cultural explanations is that they keep society's more structural or systemic issues off the table. Mass unemployment should give us occasion to question the efficacy of work as a basis for social inclusion and solidarity" (p. 100). We must conceptualize our inherent value within our communities as something that is unrelated to our value in a capitalist labour market.

If we are to take risk factors for domestic homicide seriously, we must acknowledge the way in which our cultural relationship to work and the heteropatriarchal means we use to secure men's participation in a dangerous and often damaging workforce might be creating harm for all our communities. In carceral accounts of domestic homicide, we position "occupational stress" as a risk factor for domestic homicide and locate the failure inside the individual perpetrator, never once asking whether work itself is the problem. Kaba tells us that "capitalism is actually continually alienating us from each other, but also even from ourselves" (2021, p. 67). Where would Professor Merivale's colonial policies be without the fetishized objects of consumer desire? How could the colonizer have secured participation of settlers in the expansion of the colonial project without the promise of "property"? The existential insecurity experienced by domestic killers who seek to exert ultimate control over their partners when faced with occupational failure must be understood as socially and culturally situated in contemporary capitalism.

Occupational stress, beyond its role as a potential trigger for domestic homicide, must be understood as an epidemic of unacceptable proportions. If we accept that occupation, as the architecture of racial capitalism in our collective daily lives, is harmful and alienating for all of us, we can accept that the liberation and healing of the most dangerous intimate terrorists is bound up in our own liberation from the miseries of work. If we acknowledge that the same desire to possess, control and achieve security through the domination of others exists within us, as those who also harm, then we can maintain forms of allyship even with those who transgress so deeply that they become unrecognizable as our kin.

# Desmond

On January 3, 2017, Lionel Desmond bought a rifle. He changed into full camouflage gear. He parked his vehicle on a logging road close to his estranged wife and daughter's home and hiked to the home through the trees.

Police would later find the tires slashed on his wife's vehicle in the driveway.

Inside the home was his wife, Shanna, his daughter, Aaliyah, and his own mother, who was visiting for the holidays.

He entered the home and shot his wife three times. She was killed. His mother called a family member for help. By the time family arrived, Aaliyah and Brenda Desmond had also been shot and killed.[1]

Lionel Desmond was dead with an apparent self-inflicted gunshot wound.

⇜ ◊ ⇝

Testimony at an inquiry into the deaths that occurred on that day revealed a patchwork failure of domestic violence and mental health services in the rural area of Guysborough County.

Early media headlines attributed this tragedy to his PTSD diagnosis. Early news coverage featured photos of him proudly wearing his combat uniform and smiling at the camera.

His surviving family members were quick to blame the military and their lack of support for him following a particularly devastating tour of duty in Afghanistan that left him with PTSD and a head injury. Family testified that he changed significantly after returning from Afghanistan, where he had been in active gunfights with Taliban fighters and exposed to corpses.

Lionel Desmond had posted on social media about his jealousy and controlling behaviour with his wife. Shanna Desmond's sister told the media that Shanna had been afraid that Lionel would kill her. She said she encouraged Shanna to stand by her husband.

❧◆❧

As news media began to circulate coverage that featured kind words from his fellow soldiers and friends, I felt enraged. Where was the coverage about the victims? Why was he being memorialized in such a way?

There were four victims on that day, but the public only seemed interested in the services that failed one of them. As Elizabeth Renzetti pointed out in a column, the women who are victims should be seen as more than just casualties in the killer's story.[2]

I was angry and frustrated that those who were closest to the tragedy and those who covered the stories were so quick to downplay family violence as a contributing factor in the deaths. PTSD, alone, does not make someone kill their mother, partner and child.

I tweeted angrily at CBC about their misinformed reporting of his PTSD diagnosis as a cause for violence. Many veterans have PTSD and don't harm their families. The coverage was stigmatizing.

I argued that not all intimate partner homicide is caused by trauma. I argued for a multi-layered understanding of the role of stress, trauma and factors related to intimate partner violence and coercive control. I didn't say anything that hadn't already been said—and repeated over and over again—in established literature about domestic violence and PTSD.

I spoke about this publicly on a national radio show. I received death threats in all my inboxes within twenty-four hours. They even came via snail mail to my campus mailbox. Someone took the time to lick a stamp and address an envelope just to tell me that I was a worthless piece of shit.

"how dare you disrespect him in such a way—he was a veteran who served this country"

"ugly cunt, fuck you"

"I am writing to your boss and telling them to fire you—you have no idea what you are talking about"

"bitch, I know where you live"

ঌ ◊ ঌ

The men I work with in prison saw me on the news. They can't read online comments and are unaware of the backlash. They tell me they are proud of me.

I tell them that my comments weren't received well by a lot of folks in Nova Scotia.

I tell them how hard it is to talk about these issues. Settler cultures have extremely low emotional literacy. We lack the language and frameworks to account for complexity. As far as the public is concerned, there is a binary between sane/insane; good/bad. You're either crazy and not guilty for your crime, or you're not crazy and an evil person for doing something terrible.

Surrounded by a small group of men serving life sentences for homicide, I open up about the killing of Raymond Taavel, a gay man in Halifax. He was killed by a man who was severely mentally ill, who uttered terrible homophobic slurs at Raymond before beating him to death on the sidewalk. The memorial to Raymond is directly outside the front window of the queer art space where I spend a lot of time. I walk by it almost every day. It was the place where Raymond bled out on the sidewalk and ultimately succumbed to his injuries.

We talk about how all the concepts that are relevant in the criminal justice system (guilty/not guilty; insane/sane; victim/perpetrator) are useless in understanding what makes someone kill.

I tell them I am frustrated at the discourse around Raymond Taavel's killer for the same reasons I am frustrated with what the media is saying about Lionel Desmond. In both cases, the public seems unable to acknowledge that you can be in a deep crisis and unable to control yourself but still be "sane" in legal terms. You can be a victim of a lifetime of abuse (in your childhood, your work, your community) and still be responsible for victimizing someone else. You can be suffering so intensely that you can be temporarily out of touch with reality and still be motivated by hate. I argue that Raymond Taavel died because Andre Denny never got the mental health support or addictions treatment that he needed as a young man. I also argue that he experienced terrible discrimination as a young Indigenous man in a racist rural community. Yet, he can be a victim of these things and still accountable for how hateful and abusive his behavior was.

The men nod. These are things I learned from them, after all.

Lionel Desmond, after witnessing graphic and unspeakable killing as a soldier, is a collateral victim of state violence. He's also an intimate terrorist, who punched down in response to his distress. He's also a state terrorist because he is a soldier. It's fucking complicated.

Arguments over whether someone is a victim or perpetrator just detract us from having the real conversations we need about rehabilitation, prevention, protection and healing.

One of the men in my group identifies with Desmond. He has been incarcerated for a long time. He has never used an ATM machine. He has never used a computer. He tells me that he thinks that men who are violent need to be somewhere safe.

I ask him what he means.

He says that he knows that he killed his partner because he let the ugliness of the world seep into the wounds he got as a child. He empathizes with his younger self, who was the victim of abuse, but still holds himself accountable for the violence he perpetrated decades ago. He tells me that he was as much a risk to himself as he was to the women in his life before he was incarcerated. He tells me that he figures a lot of men are just as likely to harm themselves as the people around them.

I nod. That's what the data tells us.

He tells me that we don't need to argue about whether someone is a victim or perpetrator. He tells me that he figures men who kill need saving from themselves. If we create safe places for them to heal until they can be accountable and live according to their values, we're not just protecting women. We're also protecting them from harming themselves in the ways the world has trained them to.

It strikes me that his observation is one of the most pragmatic and generous perspectives I have heard in debates about perpetrator rehabilitation. I make a mental note to disengage from arguing with online comments and focus more squarely on what incarcerated people have to say about the world.

If we're going to heal from trauma, we need to disentangle ourselves from the existential violence that is taught at every level of society. If we can find ourselves inside the tangled snarl of pain and bad ideas about masculinity and power, then we can start to tease out a pathway to safety for those who harm and those who are vulnerable to them.

That world, one where binaries of victim/offender are given up in favour of more precise and generative frameworks about safety and healing, is a long way off from where we are today.

𖡦 ◈ 𖡦

Lionel Desmond was released from the Canadian Forces in 2015. He received treatment at the Occupational Stress Injury Clinic in Fredericton and at St. Anne's Hospital in Montreal, but he left treatment early to return home to Nova Scotia.

The report of the fatality inquiry into the murder-suicide includes details about how he sought help in emergency rooms in hospitals in rural Nova Scotia but was not admitted at the time.[3]

At one point, Desmond told his wife that he had dreams of murdering her after finding her in bed with another man.

He told clinicians that he wanted to get revenge on her because he thought she was taking advantage of him financially during their separation. When pressed, he admitted that he meant "financial revenge."

Despite his mental health history, his recent separation from his wife, his obvious occupational stress and difficulty processing both his tour of duty and his newfound unemployment, he was able to buy a rifle on the day of the murders.

𖡦 ◈ 𖡦

As I write this, the inquiry is still hearing testimony.

I read parts of the testimony as it is live-tweeted by journalists and then follow up with the full transcripts as they are posted online.

As I am reading news coverage about the day's testimony, a story breaks about how commanding officers interfered with military police investigations of sexual assault within the Canadian Armed Forces. The top military commander stepped down following reports of sexual misconduct.

My Twitter feed is an absurdist collage of state and gender violence. I wonder why I am writing a book and wish, instead, that I could just project my Twitter feed in the sky like the bat symbol.

I think about the terrible experiences that soldiers have in combat. I think about what it must be like to experience that on top of being assaulted by another officer.

I think about my friend Kelly and how she was threatened and intimidated by her own peers in the police force as she worked to get justice for victims of sexual violence.

I wonder what it must feel like to be discharged from being a soldier, a broken version of yourself, and have to return to daily life after combat.

I think about how Marc Lépine tried to join the Canadian Armed Forces and was rejected.[4]

Lionel Desmond's face stares back at me, smiling, in uniform from the front page of a newspaper.

## Notes

1. Michael MacDonald, "RCMP officer testifies that Lionel Desmond was deliberate in his plan to murder family members," Canadian Press, January 29, 2020. <https://globalnews.ca/news/6478702/inquiry-into-death-of-lionel-desmond-hears-that-former-soldier-purchased-rifle-before-killing/>.

2. Elizabeth Renzetti, "Women killed by their spouses are not casualties in someone else's story," *Globe and Mail,* January 26. 2017. < https://www.theglobeandmail.com/opinion/women-killed-by-their-spouses-are-not-casualties-in-someone-elses-story/article33535098/?reqid=81a9741b-59c3-47b0-a6be-0b05812b3535>.

3. Desmond Fatality Inquiry, Transcripts, <https://desmondinquiry.ca/transcripts.html>.

4. Mary Williams Walsh, "Canadian Killer Sulked When Things Went Wrong," *Los Angeles Times,* Dec. 8, 1989. <https://www.latimes.com/archives/la-xpm-1989-12-08-mn-293-story.html>.

# Towards Transformative Justice and Collective Survivorship

"When you are under the coercive control of an abuser or in an interpersonal violent relationship leaving doesn't feel like a safe or achievable option."
— FKA Twigs, Instagram @fkatwigs, December 11, 2020

"Data from intimate partner violence fatality reviews shows that a significant number of homicide victims have no involvement with the legal system, criminal or civil, before they are killed; one study found that only half of the women killed by intimate partners had had contact with the criminal system in the year before they were killed."
— Leigh Goodmark, 2018, loc. 2747

I'm sitting in my cluttered office, imagining you, the reader. I am trying to think about what I want to say to you. I want to tell you that I know how to fix things. I don't. I have ideas, but I want to hash them out with you, the way I talk them over with folks I am in community with on the unceded territory I call home.

Mostly I am imagining what kinds of ideas you might have after reading what I have written so far. I imagine that much of what I have written is not new to you, and I wonder how you feel about it all... I wish we were in the same room, so we could pause. Make a cup of tea. Then talk about where we go next, together.

I am distracted by Twitter, again.

A police officer who does diplomatic detail for the British government was just arrested in connection to the kidnapping and murder of a young woman named Sarah Everard in England.[1] Public shock and disbelief are echoing across the digital mediascape as I write this chapter in March 2021. Feminists are decrying poor public responses that have responsibilized women for their safety by telling them not to walk after dark, which we've encountered a thousand times before.

As always, mainstream feminist responses that I read, scrolling through social media, offer little analysis on the role of a police officer in the suspected killing of the young woman in England. I get up and make a cup of tea for myself.

☙ ◊ ❧

Despite the fact that men are killed by homicide at a much greater rate than women and girls, the anti-femicide movement continues to frame gender-based violence as the result of men's violence against women, and the conversation about gender and homicide ends there. Flood's research into gender-based violence with men in Australia shows us that to understand men's violence against women, we must examine the structure and fabric of their relationships with each other. Flood's research demonstrates that in men's violence against women, "other men are the imagined audience" (2007, p. 348). The intent of their violence is to secure masculine status and strengthen bonds with other men in institutionalized heteropatriarchal society.

If men's violence against women is mediated by their relationships in heteropatriarchal institutions, then men's violence against each other should be part of the conversation about domestic homicide. National and global data consistently demonstrate that men are far more likely to suffer violent deaths at the hands of each other than women are (McEvoy and Hideg, 2017). For example, globalized data shows that women make up 16 percent of violent deaths, where men represent 84 percent of the victims of violence. Interestingly, where income inequality is reduced, homicide rates go down (Szalavitz, 2018), but domestic homicide rates remain fairly stable (McEvoy and Hideg). This is especially true of former European colonies, such as Australia, Canada and the United States, pointing to the fact that income inequality and rates of men's interpersonal violence are not the only drivers of domestic homicide. There are socio-cultural factors that drive domestic and non-domestic homicide as a reaction to extreme stress and crisis.

Carceral feminism wants to imprison more and greater numbers of men to make us safer. But incarcerating violent men will not stop others from learning to be violent and killing each other, their kin or themselves. The existential insecurities brought on by racial capitalism will continue to present annihilation of self and others as a reaction to economic or occupational stress. Unless we deal with the socio-cultural causes of homicidal response to distress, we will not stop this violence.

What if we took calls to examine men's violence seriously and looked at the *causes* of their violence with abolitionist care and attention? In this book, I try to do just that, to focus on the most dangerous form of intimate partner violence and trace where it historically emerged through processes of colonialism, the formation of the nuclear family and the rise of racial capitalism. When we examine the genealogy of coercive control relations, occupational stress and the reification of the hypermasculine roles of police and military, we see that the process of European colonial state-making was founded on the very same pattern of relations that lead to domestic homicide today.

Misogyny is an effect of settler colonialism. We can't talk about one without implicating the other. The acquisition of land and territory was achieved through the patriarchal possessive logic of white supremacy in colonialism. The land was/is treated as an *object* to exploit and possess in our social and economic system. Black people were treated as "objects" to be bought and sold by white landowners and continue to face dehumanizing coercion, terror and violence at the hands of police. Advocates against femicide argue that women are killed in domestic homicides because they are "objectified" and seen as "property."

The common thread in all these coercive control relations is objectification produced by systems of private property and consumer capitalism. Men take up the heteropatriarchal expectations of "work" and conflate their identity with their value in a capitalist market that creates existential insecurity through changes to the global marketplace, rising unemployment and fiscal collapse. Income inequality, produced and maintained by racial capitalism, is the biggest statistical predictor of high homicide rates (Szalavitz, 2018). In places with high income inequality, "men have little hope of a better future for either themselves or their kids, [and] fights over what little status they have left" lead to tragic outcomes (Szalavitz, 2018). When these tragedies occur, we simply do not have adequate services for survivors of family violence. The cycle of state violence continues to reverberate, structuring our intimate and familial relations.

Abuse and coercion reach far back through generations in communities that are either rural and underserved or urban and overpoliced. Many of us still think that expanding the scope of the carceral system to include ever more "crimes" and infractions will somehow make this change. Expanding the scope and powers of the police will only lead to increased criminalization of Black and Indigenous Canadians. Police and prisons are not the answer to domestic homicide. Ending the conditions that give rise to domestic homicide requires transformation from carceral feminism to an anti-racist and anti-capitalist feminism that takes possessiveness, coercion and objectification seriously.

In the preceding pages, I opened frameworks for thinking about domestic homicide in the context of state violence in settler colonialism and our occupational misery in racial capitalism. The most dangerous forms of intimate partner and family violence force us to think carefully through the pragmatics of a community-based response and the dangers we may encounter when we intervene. Police may pose a danger to our collective well-being, but so do volatile coercive partners who pose a risk to the survival of their partners, children or bystanders who may be in their path. Currently, in many radical abolitionist movements, community accountability circles are the go-to strategy for gender-based violence (Incite!, 2016; Bierria, Kim and Rojas, 2010; Russo, 2018). State and intimate terrorists require a different strategy for intervention than accountability circles or community-based approaches to nurturing accountability for change with one's peers and kin. The danger posed by coercive control abuse requires an abolitionist re-orientation towards collective self-defence and insurgent collaboration with killers and those who have harmed and healed.

In this chapter, I want to consider implications for intervention, prevention and transformation of the conditions that lead to domestic homicide. I explore how strategic abolitionist approaches to understanding risk and safety while intervening in family violence can help keep us all safer when are doing this work. I suggest two preliminary concepts that could provide frameworks for prevention and transformation of the conditions produced by settler colonialism and racial capitalism: collective survivorship and insurgent love. Ultimately, I emphasize that abolitionist strategies against family violence make the most sense when we *listen* to the significant majority of survivors who don't want to involve police (Ryan et al., 2021; Singer, 2012; Goodmark, 2018). As communities, we must be prepared to intervene in both situational couple violence and more dangerous intimate terrorist relations as we work to defund and dismantle policing as the only available option for survivors of family violence. By "we," I am including my abolitionist allies and any current or former carceral feminists who might be willing to become traitors to the carceral state.

Brenda Desmond called her brother in the minutes before she was shot by her son. In a rural, underserved Black Scotian community in a province with a long history of anti-Black racism and mistreatment by police, it makes sense that 911 was not her first call. As families, friends, communities, we need to be ready take those calls and feel confident that we have strategies to protect ourselves and others when we intervene.

## Intervention: The Dangerous Work of Healing Justice for State and Intimate Terrorism

Stephen Wentzell phoned the police when he heard intimate partner violence in a neighbour's home. A few weeks later the neighbour he reported to the police for beating his partner showed up on his doorstep in a rage.

Wentzell, a gay man, started recording as the man who was beating him called him a faggot and taunted him. Wentzell screamed for help. "Help from *who*?" the man responded as he was beating Wentzell. He repeatedly punched Wentzell in the skull, leaving him with a concussion.[2]

Police charged the abuser with assault, but he was never charged for the intimate partner violence incident. He was released back to his home.

Police sent out a public response, saying that they do not have the ability to evict someone from their home even if they viciously attacked their neighbour. Wentzell told media he is terrified to be in his yard and fears having guests over to his home.

The voice of the perpetrator from the video stays with me.

"Help from *who*?"

Exactly.

❧◆❧

Many of the cases of intimate partner violence we become familiar with through our peer groups represent the less dangerous forms of situational couple violence. Those who live with an intimate terrorist are not likely to be part of collective movements for justice or social change. They are often isolated and alienated from the broader community—but we mustn't forget that they are here, with us, in our communities. We must acknowledge that there is violence happening that we don't know about. For survivors of high-risk family violence, keeping the violence a secret can mean the difference between life and death. This is not the type of relationship we hear about in public calls for community accountability when we have an abuser in our midst. However, when we do find ourselves in a position to support someone who is living with intimate terrorism, this kind of violence can pose tremendous danger to all parties when outsiders try to intervene (National Coalition Against Domestic Violence, 2020).

Feminist abolitionist movements for community accountability (Incite!, 2016; Bierria, Kim and Rojas, 2010; Russo, 2018) involve groups of peers in structured "pods" (Barrie, 2020) or circles (Kim, 2018) who work under the direction of a survivor to support and coax an abusive person to shift their harmful behaviour to more healthy ways of coping with distress. Alisa Bierria et al. connect this contemporary history of using community accountability practices as a form of resistance against state violence in the prison industrial complex. They point out that, "despite their inconsistent and at times ineffective responses to domestic and sexual violence, communities have left a meaningful legacy" (2010, p. 4) They argue that these "responses have *persevered* and are far more common than criminal responses are. Community accountability practices are revealed in family oral histories and in intimate kitchen-table and backroom storytelling" (p. 4). Community accountability, as articulated by Incite! (2016) and others (Chen et al., 2016), is any strategy or practice designed to address violence or abuse that creates forms of justice and safety that are not reliant on police, prisons or their associated network of state agencies. Community accountability practices have been and continue to be an important tool in abolitionist movements against violence. These approaches can work well for some forms of violence, such as situational couple violence and some sex offences against children (Generation Five, 2007).

However, coercive control relationships are not the kind of abusive relationship that can safely progress through what we currently understand as community-based approaches to healing and behaviour change. Johnson points out:

> Some of the interventions indicated for situational couple violence might actually pose a danger to a victim of intimate terrorism. For example, couples counseling (often recommended as a remedy for communication skills deficits) would place a victim of intimate terrorism in the position of going into counseling sessions with a man who may kill her for telling the truth. (2008, p. 75)

I have had experience working with folks in community where the only safe approach was to collude with them in keeping the violence a secret. In one case, myself and others were forced, after hearing about frightening acts of violence and coercive control in a friend's relationship, to continue to engage with the abuser as if nothing had happened. If we reacted with disdain or fear, the abuser would know that the survivor told others about the abuse. This would have placed the survivor at greater risk for violence.

In instances where an abusive partner might lose their job if a public callout materializes, the conditions become significantly more dangerous for the survivor. Where many "callouts" (Brown, 2020) work to try and topple abusers from positions of power, survivors may rightly perceive that public condemnation and job loss could create a volatile crisis in their relationship and put them in grave danger. Community accountability practices that rely on the involvement of peers, friends or family are not appropriate for high-risk family violence. Some of the strategies that have been developed for addressing sexual violence, harassment and situational couple violence through feminist accountability practices may pose lethal danger for those at the highest risk for domestic homicide. Secrecy and safety-planning practices that don't rely on broad community involvement are safer options for survivors and bystanders who seek to intervene.

It's important to acknowledge that some survivors in radical communities that promote feminist accountability practices may engage in callouts about other abusers but may need to keep the violence in their own lives secret. Lena Palacios speaks about her journey as a survivor, from movements for vigilante justice against her abusers to developing her own "sixth sense" about the "immoral affective heart of the carceral state" (2016, p.

94), which informs emerging movements for feminist transformative justice praxis. Those of us who are survivors of state and intimate violence must negotiate the affective mess of violence in ways that struggle for coherence in neat and tidy but abstract rhetoric about violence and justice.

It is not the intention of this book to create a moral hierarchy in which pacifist, transformative movements for the healing of killers are positioned as the ultimate moral goal. Palacios asserts that "impolite, outlaw, and renegade theory helps to reveal the contradictory and disjunctive processes" (p. 96) that draw neat boxes around what is carceral and what is transformative. This is a binary I seek to resist. It is my intention to remain pragmatic around the utility of our transformative justice projects in consideration of those who pose the greatest danger to us: state terrorists—such as cops and soldiers—and intimate terrorists, our kin who pose the greatest danger to those who live in the shadows of ongoing coercion and abuse. Community accountability practices, many of which rely on the unpaid labour of other survivors or community members who are vulnerable in other ways, must acknowledge the dangerous implications of engaging with intimate terrorists, who may be in the depths of a crisis that renders our attempts at support invisible to them.

Developing community strategies to respond to intimate terrorism requires us to engage in practices of *risk assessment* to keep the conditions of this unpaid healing labour as safe as possible. Pathways to justice might not always be linear or coherent, but we must be clear on when we are dealing with high-risk violence and err on the side of caution. We need to know what kind of violence we are intervening in before we put ourselves on the line. adrienne marie brown (2020) argues that abolitionist movements need a "glossary" of harm that will guide us into knowing when and how to intervene when harm has taken place. She outlines various aspects of harm, but abuse is defined as a single category.

I argue for a dual category of intimate partner and family violence that distinguishes between when it is safe to heal together, using existing community accountability practices (Kaba and Hassan, 2019) and the involvement of peers, and when we need strategies for collective self-defence and protection for survivors and those who are working to intervene. When an abuser is actively or desperately clinging to strategies of coercive control and violence as their primary means of possessing their partners, they are not in a place that is receptive to healing. We can't do a community accountability process with a cop, and we can't do an accountability process with an intimate terrorist. When the threat of homicide is high and the power imbalance between abuser and survivor is stark and clear, we need other avenues to safety.

ᕦ ◇ ᕤ

I met Karyn at a community meeting in Toronto. Her son was killed by a cop.

He had been struggling with a drug addiction that he had fallen into to find respite from symptoms of undiagnosed mental illness. His family had tried—over and over again—to help him find treatment for both the mental illness and the addiction. For a while, things were looking up. He received a bipolar disorder diagnosis and was being treated for it, along with methadone for his drug problem.[3]

"Two days later, Trevor went out to go get some cigarettes for himself and others who couldn't drive to go get cigarettes. He went out and he was arrested for failure to appear for addictions treatment, which he was getting his methadone in the hospital, so. The missed link there was between his probation officer and Trevor because she didn't realize he was in treatment, unfortunately, so she put out a bench warrant and that's what happened. So, he was arrested again, and it took three days before he could get the right medications for his methadone, so he was in withdrawal. The second and third day, it was really bad, his mental health meds that he was on that were helping. So that pretty much put him back quite a bit."

He moved in with his mom. He had tried numerous times to take his own life. Once he parked a car on train tracks and went to sleep. He was saved by a passerby who pushed the vehicle off the tracks.

One night he went out and never came home. Police said he tried to rob a drugstore. He walked directly into the gunshot. They didn't want to let her see the body.

She founded a group called Affected Families of Police Homicide to work with other families left grieving after a police homicide. We are talking about some of the failed police reform strategies in Toronto. She thinks that some good people try to be police officers and end up getting chewed up and changed by the culture of policing. She thinks their training is deeply harmful. She also thinks the force attracts the wrong people. It's violent. And hypermasculine.

She points out that, in Toronto, there is no other option to get a $100,000 paycheck with only a high school diploma. Unemployment is high. University tuition is rising. The cost of living in Southern Ontario is through the roof. Everyone needs to work. And to get paid a living wage.

She tells me that police have been invited to the table at various community meetings with mental health advocacy organizations and with families like hers. She tells me that they often show up in full tactical gear. She recounts one story where a cop in attendance left families and community members shaken:

"And there were so many people that were affected by this police officer walking in all his grays, wearing swat with a big gun strapped to his leg. He wanted to be part of the conversation. No!"

You can't collaborate for justice with your abuser when they bring a gun to the table.

## Community-Based Risk Assessment, Safety Thresholds and Safety Planning

As discussed earlier in this book, risk factors for domestic homicide are well known, and many of these deaths are preventable if we can identify the red flags. Community-based risk assessment is imperative to fostering pathways to safety for those who are in the greatest danger and those who seek to intervene. Community-based risk assessment shifts the responsibility for assessing danger from police to community-based movements and organizations that are in contact with survivors on a regular basis. Police employ well-established research on high-risk family violence through various types of risk "checklists" when they respond to domestic violence calls (Campbell, 2016). Community-based risk assessment would see the practice extended outside of policing so that survivors can inform those they are closest to of the level of danger they are experiencing. These checklists can be used and adapted by community-based movements to assess and react to differing risks for lethality in a family violence context. As organizers working outside carceral systems to build safer communities, we need to know when to undergo a community accountability process with an abusive partner to assist them in changing their behaviour, or when to engage in harm reduction and safety planning in a high-risk situation. Understanding the difference between these two possible pathways to safety is vital to our individual and collective survival.

For community-based mobilizations against family violence that want to engage in risk assessment before intervening, I offer the following list of "red flags," drawn from feminist domestic violence research (Campbell et al., 2003; Campbell, 2016a). Risk assessments can assist community organizers in developing their own "safety thresholds" for when and how to engage with an abuser, if at all. A safety threshold would be the place at which the number of red flags for lethal violence indicates a need for something other than a community accountability practice that relies on peer-based intervention with the abuser. Data (Campbell et al., 2003) shows that these danger assessment questions are relevant to both heterosexual and same-sex abusive relationships.

- Is the survivor terrified to tell you about the abuse? Do they need you to keep it secret?
- Is the survivor trying to leave? Is the relationship dissolving, or is there a recent separation?
- Does the abusive partner show extreme jealousy or possessiveness?
- Has the abusive partner ever strangled or tried to strangle the survivor?
- Does the abusive partner have access to firearms? Have they ever used a weapon of any kind to make threats?
- Is the abusive partner escalating their violence or attempts to control?
- Has the abusive partner threatened to harm pets, children or others the survivor cares about?
- Is the abusive partner suicidal? Or are they using threats of suicide to try and hold on to the relationship?
- Is the abusive partner facing recent or ongoing unemployment or high levels of occupational stress?
- Is the abusive partner using alcohol or drugs regularly and in ways that impair their function?

- Does the abusive partner stalk or follow the survivor or snoop through their private messages, their phone? Do they seem to always know where the survivor is?
- Are there children present in the home, and are any of these children not biologically related to the abusive partner?
- Is the survivor pregnant, or were they pregnant at any point while experiencing escalating levels of abuse?
- Has the abusive partner ever made threats to kill the survivor?
- Has sexual assault taken place in the relationship?

This list is adapted from Jacquelyn Campbell's work at <www.dangerassessment.org>. It is a blending of the same-sex and heterosexual relationship questionnaires created by Campbell and others. If the answer to any of these questions is yes, then there is elevated danger for domestic homicide or severe violence. The higher the number of "yes" responses, the greater the risk of homicide.

The presence of any one of these red flags in an abusive relationship should caution community members from trying to intervene without careful safety planning and consent from the survivor. In cases where one or more of the answers to these questions is yes, then supportive friends and family might want to consider safety planning with the support of a secure shelter or domestic violence advocates who are familiar with safe housing options for survivors trying to leave a high-risk relationship. Safe housing means a place that has kick-proof doors and/or bulletproof windows. Many secure shelters are in secret locations and are built and maintained to withstand stalking or weapons-related assaults from an aggrieved partner. These shelters are not always available.

*Safety planning* is the process of working with a survivor to ensure that they are able to leave safely or have the option to leave if they choose to do so. In some cases, this might mean keeping a stash of clothes, cash and copies of important documents like a passport or driver's licence in another location with a friend. It might mean arming oneself. It could mean instituting a safe word to be used on the phone or in messages with a friend or family member who knows what it means. It is likely to mean acknowledging that leaving the relationship might cause lethal violence and planning for this possibility.

For survivors who want to stay in a high-risk relationship, supportive friends and family might consider a *harm-reduction* approach, which might involve checking-in with the survivor secretly and/or maintaining a non-judgemental approach to their decision-making, which will ensure that they don't disappear out of shame or guilt for staying in their relationship. Community mobilization to raise awareness around the harms of stalking would also help those who are affected to recognize the dangers of this type of behaviour from a current or ex-partner. Stalking or snooping, like that demonstrated by Nicholas Butcher in the days preceding his attack on Kristin Johnston, are rarely recognized as indicators of serious boundary-crossing or controlling behaviour. When friends or family become aware of any of these red flags, it is an indicator that safety planning (rather than confrontation with the abuser) is needed to ensure everyone's safety.

For many feminist abolitionists, especially Black women, who have been organizing community-based movements for accountability for decades, these considerations are not new. However, where community-based mobilizations for justice require that more folks get involved in confronting the violence of the state, these considerations should be made clear to those who may not have years of experience working with survivors of gender-based violence. Elders in these movements for justice and those with experience must be able to share information that is vital for new participants, who may not be clear on what abuse is, how it is perpetuated or how to intervene in it safely.

## The Suicidal or "Emotionally Dependent" Abuser

As discussed in this book, police often do not view a "civil reputable" or "emotionally dependent" abuser as a credible threat to a survivor's safety. This is the case with community intervention, too. The same problems exist when we try to intervene without knowledge and experience about how abusers operate and how they present, especially when they may be suicidal or in obvious distress. Our instincts when faced with a needy, insecure or suicidal person who has been accused of abuse is to focus on their safety so they don't try to take their own life. We may believe the survivor, but we can't help but be impacted by the distress signals that an emotionally dependent or suicidal abuser might be giving off.

Community-based movements against family violence must develop tools to respond to suicidal distress while also keeping bystanders and partners safe. When we are in contact with a suicidal person who appears to be in distress over the end of the relationship and may be engaging in stalking behaviours, we need to be immediately concerned for the safety of the person they are stalking. Threats of suicide often escalate when a survivor is trying to leave and can indicate a dangerous spiral of shame and rage that can end in devastating violence. Conner et al. (2002) examined suicide threats and attempts in family-violence court cases where survivors were requesting protective measures. They found that suicidal behaviour or manipulative threats of suicide were prevalent in times when violence escalated in the relationship. Suicide attempts or threats can indicate a period of desperation and, when coupled with other high-risk behaviours, can indicate a danger for domestic homicide even if there is no prior physical violence in the relationship. Suicidal impulses may mean that more than one person is in danger.

A need to keep partners safe from their abuser's suicidal distress may mean violating confidentiality for those the abuser has confided in. This presents a tricky problem for folks who work closely with members of our community who are harmful. Although privacy, refuge and confidentiality are required for some forms of healing and accountability, maintaining the confidentiality of the harmful person over the safety of their partner and family can have tragic outcomes. For those who are providing frontline and direct support to someone in suicidal distress who also appears to be obsessing over a current or former partner or demanding to be in contact with a partner who has asked for space—this should raise a red flag. In these cases, suicide intervention and support should be provided without any involvement with the former partner, and this should be made clear at every step. Those who are intervening should safety-plan, assess for the presence of weapons, stay in groups of two or more and ensure that they are receiving support before and after an intervention with a suicidal person who might be abusive.

## Not All Abusers Are the Same: Child Victims Need Us to Understand Their Abusers

One of the most powerful and oft-cited works in abolitionist writing about family violence is a report released by Generation Five in 2007 entitled *Toward Transformative Justice: A Liberatory Approach to Child Sexual Abuse and Other Forms of Intimate and Community Violence*. Generation Five draw important links between generational violence and state violence;

they advocate for transformative healing strategies that don't rely on the carceral system for families and communities. The authors note that this work was informed by their collective participation in "developing strategic responses to incidents of child sexual abuse" (p. 3).

Although this report was a foundational piece in helping abolitionist movements think through community-based healing responses to sexual and family violence, it does not take into account some major differences in how various types of intimate partner violence unfold in families and how those who cause harm are not a homogeneous group. For example, perpetrators of child sexual abuse are some of the most receptive to healing programs, with remarkably low recidivism rates in the Canadian correctional system when they receive appropriate healing services (Wilson et al. 2009). Since 1994, in Canada, advocates for prison justice and community safety have been running transformative healing circles for perpetrators of child sexual abuse with great success. Many of the founders of this movement were connected to Mennonite and Quaker abolitionist organizing in Canada, along with Ruth Morris (2000) and others, who used "family case conferencing" and circles of support and accountability to avoid the harms of the adversarial criminal justice system throughout the 1980s and 1990s. In my own work with perpetrators of child sexual abuse, I have observed a great willingness to take accountability and receptivity to being welcomed back into community with others who are part of their accountability process.

There are very different motivations for engaging in different types of sexual and family violence. For intimate terrorists, there is neither a tradition nor any evidence that community-based healing strategies are effective. In fact, these approaches have been shown to create more risk for survivors. Child dependents who are subjected to the abuse of an intimate terrorist are at high risk for death or severe injury. As discussed previously, threats of violence to children in these relationships are often used as a control tactic. The presence of elders or children in a home with a coercive control partner requires an approach that is sensitive to the needs of intimate bystanders, even if they aren't directly subjected to coercive physical abuse. It's important to note that the genealogy of the "pod" approach, pioneered by the Bay Area Transformative Justice Collective and others in Oakland, emerged from work against child sexual abuse, which cannot be easily translated to work on high-risk intimate partner violence. Thinking carefully through the needs of survivors, the surviving kin of deceased victims and the healing needs of offenders requires us to become more attentive to differences in pathways for healing as they relate to different forms of abuse.

## From Child Welfare to Family Support

A major barrier for families to access services that could help them heal from domestic homicide, or prevent an escalation of violence in the future, is a long and racist tradition in child welfare practices in Canada. Cindy Blackstock (2007) and others (Baskin, 2012; Contenta, 2016) identify pervasive racism in child abuse and neglect investigations. For Indigenous Peoples, the child welfare system represents a continuation of the devastating practices in the residential school system. In Ontario, "Aboriginal children are also 168 per cent more likely to be taken from their homes and placed into care," and "black children are 40 per cent more likely to be investigated for abuse or neglect than white children, and 18 per cent more likely to have maltreatment confirmed" (Contenta, 2016). In rural communities where an abusive parent is known to be armed and dangerous, neighbours may fear reprisal if they report child abuse to the authorities. Emerging evidence from the inquiry into the Portapique shooting demonstrates that many knew about the violence in the shooter's childhood home, but no one was able to come to the aid of the shooter's mother or her child.

Parents rightly fear their children being taken away. They fear loss of income or homelessness if their abusive partner is arrested. They also fear reprisal if they cooperate with the authorities. As the Alliance for Men and Boys of Colour (Philpart, 2020) points out, child welfare policies must drastically change if we are to stop the cycle of violence in all our communities. There are effective precedents for wraparound family services and survivor-led programs for survivors of violence. In San Joaquin, California, the Stockton Recovery Center provides free mental health and case management services to survivors of traumatic events, including bullying, sexual assault, trafficking, domestic violence, mass shootings and more. They provide one-on-one therapy, group programs, outreach for hospital and home visits and culturally appropriate programs that reflect the values and practices of the diverse cultures in San Joaquin. Their programs include a racial justice curriculum and provide specialized services for youth, elders and entire families. In Toronto, the Gatehouse is a survivor-led peer support and advocacy organization for adult survivors of child sexual abuse. They provide group programs and advocacy for children who are in contact with police during investigations and host a Transforming Trauma conference each year that brings together frontline workers and survivors to discuss transformative strategies for reducing harm in our communities. They run programs with the leadership of survivors and include culturally specific programs that are in the appropriate language and create safety from racism or judgement from other survivors who are not from that community.

We need strategies to heal our *relations*, not just individuals who are struggling. Families need wraparound supports.

## What Do We Do With the Dangerous Few?
## Intimate Terrorists in a World Without Police

In a talk in 2019 at Berkeley, abolitionist and former public prosecutor Paul Butler (2020) made an appeal to students in attendance to think not about what kinds of dangerous people the prison locks up but about the dangers it produces. He invoked Ruth Morris's term the "dangerous few" and noted that many abolitionists agree that abolition is a long-term process and that some form of community supervision for our most dangerous kin might be necessary as we move forward with building safer societies.

In my field, I am often asked by carceral feminists how we will protect ourselves from intimate terrorists if there are no police? This question ignores the common origins of both forms of violence. If we abolish the systems that maintain the coercive control of the prison nation, we will no longer be teaching forms of intimate terrorism to our youth. By disarming, defunding, de-colonizing and de-carcerating our communities, we will prevent intimate terrorism. The question, then, is how we secure our safety in what will be a long and messy transition from settler colonialism and racial capitalism to a future that is *just* and free of white supremacist violence and misery. Furthermore, how can we help those who use coercion and control in response to their feelings of insecurity without relying on coercion and control as means of securing their participation in ending the violence? How can we balance the needs of those who cause harm with those who are at the highest risk of dying from family violence?

These are the foundational questions for abolitionist allies who want to build safety and reduce family violence and domestic homicide. Most abusive partners who engage in intimate terrorism are not yet in a place where they can heal from the trauma, occupational stress or misogynistic beliefs that cause them pain and fuel their violence. It takes time to disengage from a possessive abusive relationship—sometimes decades (Lalonde, 2020). Abusive partners who display high levels of obsessiveness or possessiveness over survivors may try to manipulate community accountability processes order to maintain contact with survivors or manipulate others into thinking they are the victim.

State and intimate terrorists present dangers to all of us. In cases where there is access to firearms or where an abusive partner is in the depths of a self-destructive or suicidal rage or shame spiral, we may face physical violence just for being in proximity to them. Our response in these high-risk scenarios must be to ensure the safety of survivors and frontline support people. Disarmament of both police and our neighbours is one pathway for transforming the conditions that produce lethal violence. Transformation requires disarmament.

࿐◊࿐

There is trouble at the Saulnierville Wharf again tonight.[4]

I am writing this final chapter as men with guns head down to the wharf in trucks.

Mi'kmaw fishers have been exercising their Treaty Rights to fish lobster in St. Mary's Bay. Angry mobs of white fishers on the Acadian shore have destroyed traps, burnt boats and set properties on fire in retaliation for those who were supporting the Indigenous livelihood fishery.

They oppose the Treaty Rights of Indigenous fishers to trap lobster outside of designated fishing seasons. They set a van on fire. Racist slurs and cans of gasoline. They are not going to let them fish.

My family is from this area. This side of my family doesn't understand calls to defund police. There are virtually no police across the vast coastal territories, island communities and villages on the shores of the Bay of Fundy.

My family is from a tiny island that can only be accessed by ferry. It is home to a multimillion-dollar fishery.

There are no surprise police raids in these communities. You can see cop cars crossing on the ferry from kilometres away.

For thirty-five years my stepdad slept next to his gun. He was captain of a successful fishing boat. He held licences for lobster, amongst other things. You might survive the icy whip of the frigid North Atlantic in December, but you still have to contend with the guys on your boat.

Men in this community struggle with addiction and deep legacies of family violence. There are no social workers in the schools. There are few who graduate from the tiny school on the island.

The ocean and the communities that line the shore are a settler frontier. Men with guns decide how things go. In this case, the settler fishers and corporations control the water. They are emboldened by federal fisheries regulations. They hold the majority of the fishing licences.

They will use guns and gasoline and whatever they can to keep settler control over the water. Although there are few police, there are many men with guns.

It's not a big leap to say that settlers have treated the water like an abusive partner treats a survivor. There isn't much life left in the water now. It's a wasteland.

As I am writing this final chapter, I recall the story of the killing of Philip Boudreau. Media dubbed it the "murder for lobster" case. Philip Boudreau was killed by fishers in another Acadian fishing community, presumably for poaching lobster. Investigation later revealed that Boudreau had been bullying and terrorizing his community for years.[5]

Men in prison told me he was killed because he pushed people too far—domestic violence, theft... They told me Boudreau was just like some other guys who went missing off a boat a few years back after they sexually assaulted a young girl in the community. "The community took care of it. Chain 'em up, drop 'em over. Done."

I'm scanning my phone for news on Saulnierville and thinking about settlers with guns.

Access to firearms is a major risk factor for domestic homicide.

We can defund police. We can disarm police. But we also have to disarm the settlers who run these remote and rural towns who are the de facto cops of their communities.

We have to disarm them all. The carceral state doesn't end at the walls of the police station, and it doesn't always wear a uniform.

## Disarmament, Collective Security and Self Defence

When violence is forced upon us, we must sometimes fight back. Frantz Fanon (1963) asserts that violence is a necessary pathway for liberation when someone has their gun to your neck. The struggle against intimate terrorism is a struggle against state terrorism. There will be times in our fight against state and intimate terrorism when we will need to defend ourselves against potentially lethal violence.

If we admit that both police and intimate terrorist abusers pose serious dangers to our collective safety, then we must, as communities, organize collective self-defence strategies that can help mitigate this danger. Self-defence strategies for intervention into high-risk relationships require long-term approaches, such as disarmament and prevention, and short-term approaches, such as safety planning and accompaniment when a survivor tries to leave a relationship. Long-term strategies for disarmament and a reduction of the numbers of guns in our communities—from police to citizens who act like them—although desperately needed, won't help in individual cases where a survivor is in danger from an armed abuser. The use of legal observers during periods of police intervention and violence or filming or documenting police and intimate partner violence has been effective in securing prosecution in the criminal justice system for individual cops (Beckett, 2021) or abusers, but it can't bring back the dead.

In both Canada and the United States, gun sales spiked during the COVID-19 pandemic (Helmore, 2021). The shooter in Portapique was not the only person responding to a time of stress and crisis by arming himself to the teeth (D'Souza, 2020). The violence and terror imparted by police and intimate terrorists in our homes and on our streets cannot always be met with pacifism. Collective self-defence strategies can help to deflect the diffusion of our energies when an abuser is not willing to disengage from abuse and violence. A focus on collective self-defence shifts attention to how we might keep ourselves safe if we find ourselves experiencing violence as bystanders or advocates.

Community movements for collective self-defence might also work to resist the ways that survivors who have acted in self-defence against intimate terrorist abusers are individually punished and incarcerated in the criminal justice system. We must not let them struggle alone. As Mariame Kaba points out, "countless Black women and trans people who act in self-defense when police fail to protect them languish in prison, denied the right to assert self-defense because our legal system has deemed they have no legitimate selves to defend" (2021, p. 110). Collective security is more powerful than individual self-defence. In Canada, we see racist legal practices enshrine the right for white people to engage in self-defence against perceived attacks in cases like the Colton Boushie murder trial, where a white landowner was found not guilty for fatally shooting an unarmed Cree youth.[6]

Although self-defence can bring fatal or legal ramifications for those engaged in community-based mobilizations against family violence, there are some successful examples of community-based security forces. Historically, movements such as Anti-Racist Action (ARA), the first incarnation of contemporary antifa movements, have offered physical security and protection from white supremacist skinheads and other threats to community safety (Clancy, 2017). Bear Clan Patrol, who are "Community People Working with the Community to Provide Personal Security," began as a response to the "ongoing need to assume our traditional responsibility to provide security to [the] Aboriginal community" and has expanded to multiple cities. They provide security through "a non-violent, non-threatening, non-judgmental and supportive manner primarily through relationship building and reconciliation" that "draws its direction solely from our traditional philosophies and practices" in Indigenous cultures that pre-existed colonial occupation of the land. Bear Clan Patrol, an Indigenous-led approach to providing community security, is just one incarnation of how abolitionist movements could conceptualize safety and security during times of crisis.

## Miklat

What do we do once the survivors of intimate terrorism are safe? What do we do with the person who threatens to kill them for leaving?

Micah Bazant and Lewis Wallace created a zine together as part of an art project about refuge and transformative justice. In the zine, they explore how concepts of "refuge" might work in movements for transformative justice. *Miklat* is a Hebrew word that refers to a "city of refuge" and is mentioned in the Torah as a space where a murderer can flee and find safety from avengers of their crime. I have observed in prisons that there is a sacredness to the kind of healing spaces that violent people can create for themselves when those who have experience and perspective on their own rehabilitation are in a position to guide and support those who are still in denial or pitying themselves in ways that prevent accountability.

I have argued (Whynacht, 2017) for adoption of forms of "compassionate containment" for those with lived experience of mental illness or attachment trauma that stems from childhood neglect or neoliberal state policies. Compassionate containment, or *miklat*, as Bazant and Wallace present it, can be part of our collective abolitionist justice toolkit if it is provided with care, skill and attention to the healing and autonomy of those who require it. Not *all* forms of containment are an extension of the prison industrial complex. Some forms of containment can represent healing for those who have survived neglect and require firm and loving forms of containment for the distress they experience (Whynacht, 2017).

Intimate partner violence requires specific and skilled treatment, treatment that is evidence-based and culturally appropriate and includes racial and gender justice components. Healing treatment cannot be the monopoly of mental health professionals who are trained to understand social problems through the lens of the individual to the exclusion of our social relations and broader social structures. Healing treatments must be strategically designed to address the socio-historical and individual causes of coercive behaviour. Residential treatment programs for depression, occupational stress and trauma will not work for this kind of violence unless it is offered through an abolitionist feminist lens that is informed by gender and racial justice. Lionel Desmond spent time in a residential psychiatric program. So did Marc Lépine. Nicholas Butcher reportedly spent time in an inpatient mental health facility. None of these programs offered skilled treatment in addressing the *causes* of misogynistic violence, nor did they collaborate with the community to ensure the safety of the surviving partners or families. The siloed nature of clinical psychiatric and psychological treatment creates barriers to the kind of holistic approach that is required for healing from coercive and controlling behaviours.

In our current mental health care system, a patient's right to privacy takes precedence over the safety of their family or the broader community. Privacy, however, can be central to a deep healing project. Constant scrutiny from media and those we are closest to can sometimes make it extremely difficult to untangle ourselves from the multitude of social forces acting upon us. Accountability doesn't mean much if it's in front of an audience, where optics can trump true self-accountability and the performative nature of an apology can represent a continuation of manipulative behaviour. If we are able to step back from abstract critiques of mandated mental health care and envision forms of compassionate containment for harm, then perhaps, drawing upon notions of refuge and healing, we can begin to demand residential treatment facilities for our most dangerous abusers.

Mechanisms for encouraging, or in some cases, mandating the participation of an abuser in a residential treatment facility might require collusion with existing state infrastructure. Use of coercion to mandate participation in a secure treatment facility, or for example, the use of GPS-tracked ankle monitors during treatment will no doubt echo the forms of coercive control abuse that a treatment program is designed to address. Forms of coercion to secure participation in a residential or secure treatment program must be used only in cases where a pattern of intimate terrorism is clear and where red flags for increased use of homicidal violence are present. Decisions on how these programs will be implemented and mandated should be led by survivors and former abusers who have demonstrated accountability for their previous abuse and been though long-term healing processes in community with others. Securing an abolitionist future requires a constant dance between the deep gravitational pull of carceral state systems and an altogether different pattern of relations set to a different tune.

If these spaces of healing and accountability for intimate terrorists involve the leadership and participation of those who have harmed in devastating ways and who have been through their own journeys of accountability and self-acceptance, they will be more effective than individualized counselling in forensic facilities. They could also produce opportunities for killers to contribute positively to their social world without being directly present in community with others. Abolitionist movements against family violence must acknowledge that containment can be compassionate in cases where violent or coercive behaviour is connected to a fear of abandonment or feelings of alienation or dispossession. Containment can help to nurture feelings of belonging and care. Containment can be compassionate when such spaces involve the creation of healthy friendships and temporary refuge away from the forces of occupation and violence in our everyday lives. Incarceration does not offer these opportunities. Incarceration is an unavoidably punitive approach that does not provide the social and affective conditions required for healing. Residential treatment facilities that are far from one's community of origin would also allow survivors to remain in their homes and feel safe while their abuser is in treatment. This kind of healing space might not prevent every domestic homicide—but it's a start.

## Boundary-Setting and Disposability

Abolitionist feminism tells us that the carceral state relies on disposability (Davis, 2003; Richie, 2012; Kaba, 2021) to fuel cycles of violence inherent to the prison industrial complex. Disposability, or the tendency to consider someone's life as worthless or beyond saving when they cause harm, allows us to view the prison as a morally acceptable liminal zone where we can banish those who have committed harm without asking questions about why they harmed in the first place. Kaba draws our attention to "new mechanisms of disposability [that] feed bodies to hungry dungeon economies" (2021, p. 62) in racial capitalism. She argues that "a system that never addresses the *why* behind a harm never actually contains the harm itself" (p. 62). A refusal to acknowledge the causes of violence allows us to scapegoat individuals for forms of violence that are taught and maintained in everyday life.

Abolitionist movements must include sustained analysis and attention to the harms of disposability in our carceral settler states, but we must also acknowledge how many survivors of family violence are the ones who are forced to redress the harms of carceral disposability and heteropatriarchal norms by leaning hard into their abuser's pain as they weather blows in pathological solidarity with their abusers. As Kaba reminds us, setting healthy boundaries and disposability are not the same thing (Dixon and Piepzna-Samarasinha, 2020). If we understand the difference, we can protect survivors without putting them at further risk.

Survivors of severe relationship violence are often the first to resist disposability. Victims of domestic homicide often resisted, albeit in a toxic and enabling way, accountability for their abusers because they understood the roots of their abuse and did not want to abandon them. Those who endure physical and sexual violence, coercion and terror in their homes often tell you about how their abusive partner has goodness in them. They are acutely aware of all the difficult experiences their partners have had—their upbringing, stress at work, feelings of low self-worth or self-loathing. Most survivors of high-risk intimate partner violence don't need to be convinced to resist disposability. In fact, the pendulum has swung too far in that direction, and survivors may feel responsible for enduring abuse from their partners because of the distress their partner feels.

Attention to disposability requires us to examine the state of our relations with all our kin. Alexis Shotwell (2018) acknowledges the importance of "claiming bad kin" as white people in the fight against white supremacy and racial capitalism. She writes in response to Christina Sharpe's (2016) call for white people to "lose your kin" as a form of refusal against kinship as a political project of whiteness that renders Black and other racialized people as property. Shotwell, however, points to the possibility of claiming harmful kin as a strategy for justice. She points out that, rather than co-opting Indigenous approaches to kinship, settlers must forge new ways of envisioning kinship with each other while also resisting white supremacist violence.

If we consider kinship through the lens of family violence, it becomes clear that we can't only understand kinship with harmful others in philosophical or moral terms. We must adopt new and radical forms of kinship that provide compassionate support for those who harm while also setting boundaries and refusing to enable further violence. We might need to sever our ties with harmful kin to save our lives and those of our children or dependents. Positioning reclaimed kinship with harmful kin as a moral good can lead to guilt and shame for survivors who set boundaries for their own survival. As bell hooks reminds us, women often bear the burden of the "love work" that calls heterosexual men into accountability. She acknowledges a prevailing logic of disposability in how to attend to our romantic relations, treating those bonds "like dixie cups" that are "disposable" (2018, p. 148). However, the "labor of love is futile only when men in question refuse to awaken, refuse growth. At this point, it is a gesture of self-love for women to break their commitment and move on" (p. 192). Again, it bears repeating that a key component to the cycle of family violence is the tendency of the survivors to take responsibility for their partner's violence against them. With this in mind, we must turn abolitionist attention to the pragmatics of harm in domestic spaces and commit to ending cycles of violence that responsibilize survivors for the violence of their abusers. When we engage in community accountability projects that place a lot of emphasis on an individual survivor's needs, we may be unintentionally replicating this broader pattern of family violence that makes the survivor responsible for their abuser's behaviour.

We can foster transformative forms of kinship in movements that advocate for change at the systems level while still refusing to take responsibility for the continued harms of an abusive family member or friend. In other words, we can claim someone as kin by supporting resources for their healing without making ourselves their healer. Refusing kinship, too, can be an act of *survival* and need not be equated with the harms of "disposability" produced by the carceral system. For many survivors, healing begins with saying no to being responsible for their abuser's care and healing. In these cases, experienced strangers in movements or organizations with history and expertise in supporting abusive people through their healing offer a better pathway for accountability than friends or family of the abuser. In a following section, I discuss how "surrogate survivors" (Lockhart and Zammit, 2005) and collective notions of survivorship as an ongoing struggle, rather than a stable or individualized identity category, can assist us in navigating the tricky line between enabling and support.

## Prevention and Transformation: Collective Survivorship and Insurgent Love

For the most part, in previous chapters, I relied on the term "survivor" to refer to those who are currently experiencing abuse in their families and relationships and the surviving family members of those who have lost their lives to domestic homicide. However, I wrote this book in honour of those who did not survive. There are many members of our kin and communities who are not here today; they should be. Centring our work on survivors is not possible when we are thinking through community-based responses to domestic homicide and the threat it presents to all of us. When a survivor has lost their life to violence, how can we implement a restorative or transformative process?

In cancer treatment literature, the term "survivorship" is used to reference survival as an ongoing process from the point of diagnosis and recognition to the end of life (National Cancer Institute). With the looming possibility of cancer returning to ravage the body, survivorship is understood not as a final destination that one can achieve, fully, but rather as an ongoing process of fighting the seeds of the disease that threaten to sprout within us, yet again, at any time. adrienne marie brown (2020) argues that cancer presents the perfect metaphor for understanding how forms of supremacy, the act of valuing some lives more than others, roots within us and can spread. It is also an excellent metaphor for the long-term impacts of losing a loved one to homicide. When someone we love is lost to state or intimate violence, we must negotiate this grief for the rest of our lives. Franz Fanon (1963) asks us to conceptualize colonization and all its brutality as forces that act upon the psyche, instilling colonial brutality in the contours of our deepest selves. When we are taught violence in everyday life, we must constantly resist the ways it will spread and take root inside our psyches. The struggle is long.

Survivorship, when understood as collective struggle that involves a commitment to heal from the pain and resist the temptation to let violence take root permanently within us, provides a framework for feminist transformative justice movements against domestic homicide.

I offer two preliminary concepts that might help to guide how we envision our praxis in preventing and transforming the conditions that lead to domestic homicide. The first is "collective survivorship," or the shared experience of negotiating the impact of losing a loved one to homicide, and the second is "insurgent love," a re-shaping of our relations with harmful kin who engage in intimate terrorism, a re-shaping that provides love and compassion while setting effective boundaries and providing protection for those who are vulnerable to their violence. I also ask, you, the reader, to consider how working with youth and children to foster relations of trust and care can provide a powerful means of transforming the conditions that give rise to domestic homicide.

## Surrogate Kinship

Family violence requires us to think through kinship as the space in which violence happens. This means our abusers and our victims are also our kin, or intimate partners. In a profoundly thoughtful manual on transformative and restorative approaches to justice, Arthur Lockhart and Lynn Zammit discuss the "relational disfigurement" of a victim to their abuser and describe how unequal power relations, the result of long-term and severe abuse, render many attempts at healing justice ineffective. They state the reasons why many feminists resist the use of restorative or transformative approaches for intimate partner and family violence: "Offenders will continue their manipulation through abject apology, and victims will do exactly what they are conditioned to do, by appearing to accept that apology" (2005, p. 33). However, in these cases, they raise the possibility of involving "surrogate victims," or kin, who have experienced the same kind of harm as the victim but have no prior abusive relationship with the offender. They assert that these relational forms of justice and accountability can be powerful and effective at rehabilitation without furthering the harms experienced by a survivor or responsibilizing them for their abuser's rehabilitation.

In Whynacht, Arsenault and Cooney (2018), we discuss an instance where, in an abolitionist theory class, I received a note from a student who had attended in a parole hearing as part of her experiential learning component of the class. The hearing was for someone convicted of child sex offences. The student disclosed that she was a survivor of this kind of violence but had never been able to forgive or move on from anger and feelings of betrayal. However, in the parole hearing she was able to hear the offender's story and learn about why he engaged in such terrible abuse of a vulnerable child. My student found that she was able to empathize with the offender and, that after reflecting for a couple of days, felt freer and more distant from her own feelings of victimization from her abuser. She explained that the distance afforded by being a stranger to the offender allowed her to hold the perspective she needed to heal and move on from her own abuse. She found the perspective she needed within another context.

I share this anecdote to emphasize that "surrogate victims" may also experience healing when they become active participants in the healing of a "surrogate abuser." In this way, collective survivorship allows us to think through how survivors and their abusive kin need not be bound by the confines of the nuclear family or their previous relations when participating in healing justice.

## Holding Space for Surviving Kin

When a neighbour, friend, family member or parent is killed through state or intimate violence, everyone who knew them is a survivor to some extent. We must all carry the burden of healing and respond to the imperatives of prevention and transformation as we work to honour the life that was lost. Although the pain and grief felt at the death of a loved one may resonate throughout their surviving kin and community, it is extremely difficult for surviving family to process grief after a domestic homicide. In almost half the cases, surviving family are forced to grieve the killer and the victim together, after the killer took their own life. Anger, betrayal, denial and shock reverberate in ways that are not linear or easy to understand. Survivors may swing wildly between excusing the killer's violence and then feeling angry with them. Survivors may blame the victim or blame themselves for not seeing the warning signs sooner. But how do you hold someone accountable who is no longer alive? Healing from this violence requires both individual and group processes that are led by folks with specific experience with domestic homicide. Surrogate abusers or survivors may provide an opportunity for the family members of a deceased victim to work through these processes.

Our carceral system is structured around determining guilt and innocence. This presents a barrier to participation of surviving family members who may want to advocate and organize for social change. Surviving family members of perpetrators may feel responsible for enabling the violence or not responding to warning signs. When there is a death, we feel guilty. We feel angry. We grieve. Feelings of guilt and shame may prevent surviving family and community members from accessing support services, especially if the crime was high profile or if the program relies on group or peer counselling with other members of the public. All our communities are in desperate need of non-judgemental, survivor-led peer support and advocacy groups for those who are grieving. Families who raised killers not only need to heal themselves, they may hold important information for us about what kinds of supports could have helped sooner. The surviving family of a killer, whether the killer is deceased or not, must be involved as active participants in projects for change.

## We Need Free, Accessible Mental Health Care

We do not have adequate public mental health care for survivors of family violence and traumatic events in Canada or the United States. Some large cities have day-treatment programs, but most publicly funded programs have long waitlists. The private health care system has a patchwork of mental health care professionals with varying skill sets and abilities to use evidence-based or culturally appropriate practices. Most victim services are provided through police or federal or provincial justice departments. The provision of these support services is entangled in and through the carceral system. These services are offered, when available, to the immediate family members of a victim. Rarely are services offered to the surviving family members of a perpetrator who has died by suicide. Rarely are these supports available for grieving friends or witnesses. Although some abolitionist activists believe that psychiatry and institutionalized mental health care should be abolished, my belief, as someone who worked in community-based mental health and is a trauma-survivor, is that this position is ableist. Although there are many problems with how mental health care is delivered, some forms of mental health treatment can be lifesaving (Whynacht, 2017).

For families and communities who have lost both the perpetrator and victim in a murder-suicide, there will be no trial, but there may be a public inquiry or death review committee. Victim assistance is often limited to short-term programs or small pockets of funding that are sparse and not likely to cover the costs associated with counselling in the private health care system. Counsellors and registered psychologists cost from $100 to $300 an hour in most jurisdictions. Jurors and members of public inquiries who are exposed to graphic photos and crime scene evidence can also experience trauma during these processes. Supports offered to them are minimal, if they exist at all, and they are usually only provided at the request of the judge. When the perpetrator survives and there is a trial, we end up in a trauma spiral where more and more members of our community become implicated in cycles of vicarious trauma, shame and guilt. We need to do better than this. Survivors deserve better. Those who seek to heal from being a victim of intimate terrorism, or from being an abusive partner, should be able to access the right programs and resources to support them in taking that step.

We need resources that support us in accepting collective responsibility. We may not be able to make amends to the deceased, but we can process grief and pain in ways that support collective change and social transformation. This goes beyond responding to individual deaths by creating a scholarship in a victim's name or memorializing them with roadside crosses or annual eulogies in the obituary section of the newspaper. Accepting collective responsibility means accepting where we personally and collectively enabled violence, forgiving ourselves for doing so and committing ourselves to collective movements to transform those conditions while we support others to make that change. Inquiries and death review committees can only tell us where our current system went wrong. Karyn Graham, founder of Affected Families of Police Homicide in Ontario, speaks about how powerful and healing it can be to sit with other families who are processing the same kind of grief. The advocacy work they do, in addition to their relationships with each other, offer ways to honour the lives that are lost to state violence. We need collective change for new systems, not tweaks to the old one. We need programs and services for entire families to help untangle the ways that coercion, violence and other enabling factors perpetuate through generations.

## Youth Work Is Abolitionist Work: Surrogate Kinship Is Care

Every killer I have known was once a youth who was struggling.

I teach in New Brunswick. Friends of mine grew up with the Portapique shooter. A friend of mine says that she felt sorry for him in university. He didn't fit in. Folks made fun of him.

We all know kids like that. Maybe we were those kids.

I lived in rural towns not too far from where he was raised. A few months before the shooting I saw a Facebook post about a puppy mill and animal cruelty bust in the area. The Society for the Prevention of Cruelty to Animals in New Brunswick has been responding to reports of animal cruelty and illegal puppy mills with increasing frequency as poor families turn to animal breeding to try and supplement insufficient income from social assistance. I sent a message to a woman in the area asking if she knew anything about the cruelty case as our family has a farm, and we might know folks who could foster large animals. She tells me that she knows the family who were just charged, for the third time in a decade, for severe and unimaginable cruelty to horses.

Unprompted, she tells me that there are children in that home. She tells me children as old as eight are still in diapers. She tells me that the younger ones don't go to school, and they appear malnourished. She tells me that she is worried for them, too. I call a friend who is a social worker. I ask the woman to report suspicions of child neglect (all the while feeling like shit because I know how bad the child welfare system is and that the kids might not fare better in foster care). I don't have any details and can't report it myself. She says it's a small town, and she doesn't want to interfere.

Half the town was willing to call the authorities on behalf of the animals. No one will make a call on behalf of the children. Even if they did, there is no guarantee that short-term foster care and being dragged away from the only attachments they have will help them. Even if child welfare does show up, the foster system is under-resourced and parents are unlikely to get adequate support for changing their behaviour.

I share this story of the children living on a farm full of cruelty, guns and neglect because it is the same kind of story I hear from many lifers who killed their partners. There are entire communities with generations of this kind of violence. There are youth today experiencing unimaginable cruelty in their homes. We may not be able to convince their families to heal, but we can become the kind of supports that show them what security, trust and care can feel like. We may not be able to disarm their abusers, but maybe we can help them become adults who won't buy a gun when they are drowning in misery and pain. We can do this by investing in youth-serving projects and programs in our communities.

Some of our most powerful abolitionist work can unfold inside the trusting relationships we forge with young people. Transformative justice can and must include youth who are struggling, whose families are struggling, whose schools are full of the kind of bullying and coercion that we are trying to prevent and transform into safer, more caring spaces. We don't need to be experts in intimate partner violence or commit to volunteering for a lengthy community accountability process with an abuser to make a difference in the life of *one* youth in our community. In the same way that surrogate victims or abusers can help us in fostering transformative healing processes after a domestic homicide, the surrogate forms of kinship that we can foster with young people who are alienated, neglected or abused in their homes can be a transformative act of care.

## Insurgent Love

Domestic homicide and the kind of abuse and misery that can precede it is a sickness brought upon us by white supremacy and maintained in racial capitalism. When I think about what has sustained the people I love through abolitionist struggles to transform this shared place we call home, I think about insurgence. I think about love. I think about how understanding unspeakable acts of violence requires us to love people we are not supposed to love, to be patient and nurture healthy relations with those who have caused great harm. I think about how resisting carceral feminism and questioning the legitimacy of the settler state always comes at a cost.

Those who do this are often sidelined or ignored within the domestic violence research industry. In *Beyond Survival: Strategies and Stories from the Transformative Justice Movement* (Dixon and Piepzna-Samarasinha, 2020), Audrey Huntley reflects on frontline organizing work with the families of missing and murdered Indigenous women in settler Canada. She discusses the importance of maintaining community databases and the inclusion of surviving family members of missing and murdered women. Their work is vital and has raised the profile of Indigenous women's vulnerability to violence since 1999 in Canada. She writes that "what still distinguishes us from other people who do this work was the understanding that settler colonialism [is] the inherent root of the violence" (loc. 722). This radical perspective alienated them from other organizations and movements for justice for Indigenous women in Canada, where those who received government funding feared a loss of these funding streams if they were to call the legitimacy of the Canadian state into question. She writes that, at various times, they considered deaths by suicide to be "death by colonialism," where the bullying, pain and distress caused by settler colonialism and the institutions it upholds caused further loss of life in addition to homicide. This project, like countless others who are using feminist transformative justice practices for Black and other racialized women, recognize the structural causes of state and intimate violence. Naming, resisting and fighting back against the state is a form of insurgency.

Accepting the prevalence and dangers of high-risk intimate partner violence and domestic homicide is a test to our commitment to abolition. It requires us to grapple with the real and present dangers we live with every day. It requires us to admit that even if we defund, disarm and dismantle the police, legions of settlers will turn up with their guns and militias and enact the same kinds of injustice and violence we are fighting so hard against. Accepting that "the dangerous few" are many and multiple reminds us of the dangers of this work of transformation. It reveals how deep and resistant the architecture of colonialism is within all of us as we remain committed to forms of capitalism that leave us exhausted, impoverished and struggling. We cannot escape the haunting legacies of domestic homicide unless we take seriously what it would mean to abolish work—occupation—as the central organizing feature of our lives. As frightening as it might be for some to think about what it would mean to abolish police while we face threats to our safety and survival in our own homes, we must admit that the dangers we encounter at home and the existence of police in their current formation are symptoms of the same problem.

Yet, how do we intervene, without coercion and with care and compassion, when someone threatens our very survival? Is this even possible? The answers to these questions need to come from collective organizing and experimentation in our neighbourhoods. There is no single answer.

For me, answering this question means conceptualizing love and justice as an act of insurgence, when most of us have learned love through a language of subservience.

Insurgent love understands that care requires love, but transformation might require upheaval and destruction of previous relations.

It's tricky to do those two things at the same time. But it's vital.

When I reflect upon what I have learned working closely with those who have killed their partners or loved ones, it strikes me that the very heart of intimate terror relations is one of "disfigurement," an unequal balance of power that is so beautifully discussed by Lockhart and Zammit (2005). Domestic homicide is the act of killing those you are supposed to love, or *do love*, albeit in some profoundly disfigured ways. Many of those who lost their lives to this violence *did* love the people who killed them. This is especially true for the children of parents who killed them.

Working with those convicted of these crimes has taught me that there are ways to love and care for someone who is violent—without allowing them to continue their abuse. Acknowledging this has forced me to understand kinship and care as something that can happen collectively, in distant or intimate ways, in ways that assert protection and safety. Accepting this has required me to untangle everything I have learned about love in the heteropatriarchal settler state I was born in. I have been forced to question the ways I sacrificed my safety, at various times, for those I love.

Love, as insurgency, is the antidote to martyrdom.

Martyrdom through state violence is what the state wants us to valorize and aspire to. We expect pomp and pageantry in military funerals. They want us to sacrifice ourselves for love and country. Martyrdom, or the practice of putting oneself in harm's way for the people we love, is a continuation of the relational disfigurement of coercive relations. Martyrdom, in spaces of love and intimacy, is what settler colonialism and racial capitalism demands of us. We need not endure harm, in the financialized marketplace, in our relations with police, in our relations with each other, to make up for the ways that our partners are wounded. Careful attention to the conditions of our labour in transformative justice projects for domestic homicide must acknowledge that martyrdom is a continuation of the cycle of abuse.

The Snowbirds, the Canadian air force squadron that uses tightly choreographed flight patterns to awe audiences during air force recruitment efforts, flew over Canadian skies just a few weeks after the Portapique shooting in what was dubbed Operation Inspiration. They were trying to "lift the morale of the country." During Operation Inspiration, Captain Jennifer Casey was killed when her jet crashed.

If, when seeking to make a positive impact in our communities in the fight against family violence, we accept the dangers inherent to intimate terrorism, assess risks, plan for safety and work collectively to respond to the danger, we need not end up like Captain Casey. We need not be martyrs as we seek to disarm, defund, de-colonize and dismantle.

My understanding of love as insurgence came from working with those who have harmed, specifically youth who were transitioning out of juvenile detention facilities and struggled to feel as if they were capable of being anyone other than the bully or killer that they had become to their communities. I learned, through working with them, that setting boundaries opens up space for them to be a different version of themselves. When coercion doesn't work, we have to try something else to obtain the love and security we desperately need. Setting boundaries makes space for someone to grow in a different direction.

Love, *as insurgence*, asserts that setting boundaries and saying no to harm is act of care.

Insurgent love, as a collective practice, reminds us that self-defence or community supervision for those who are dangerous can be an act of compassion rather than an expression of disposability.

Love, *as insurgence*, disrupts coercive relations and fights for a future that is defined by care rather than coercion.

Insurgent love asks for *just* relations with those we love the most.

Insurgent love, as the practice of saying no to coercion, is an act of self-love, too.

This understanding of love, while it may not be meaningful or genera-tive for every reader of this book, has been profoundly helpful for me in understanding my own relationships with people who are harmful and have harmed me. Understanding love as an act of insurgence has helped me to question my relations with others and given me permission to fight back when I need to save myself from harm and coercion. Saidiya Hartman writes: "Under heteropatriarchy, violence and rape are the terms of order, the norm; they are to be expected. So how does one lust after or relate to or want or love another? How does one claim the capacity to touch when touch is, in so many instances, the modality of violence?" (2020). Domestic homicide and the intimate terrorist relations that so often precede it beg us to sit with what Hartman is asking of us—by "us," I mean, those of us who are invested in the dismantling of settler colonialism and racial capitalism. Love, as insurgence, holds space for the renegotiation of what it means to be kin to one another, to share homes, to share our love and lives with each other.

## Notes

1. Ellen Peltier, "London Police Officer Pleads Guilty to Murdering Sarah Everard," *New York Times,* July 10, 2021. <https://www.nytimes.com/2021/07/09/world/europe/sarah-everard-wayne-couzens-murder-guilty.html>.
2. Graeme Benjamin, "Halifax man shares video of his alleged assault by man he reported for suspected domestic abuse," *Global News*, September 28, 2020. <https://globalnews.ca/news/7359917/halifax-man-shares-video-of-alleged-assault/>.
3. Jim Rankin, "Karyn Greenwood-Graham: 'I wish I'd been able to see that video,'" *Toronto Star*, Oct. 15, 2013. <https://www.thestar.com/news/insight/2013/10/15/karyn_greenwoodgraham_i_wish_id_been_able_to_see_that_video.html>.
4. This link provides excellent analysis into the ongoing disputes in Saulnierville, NS: Mercedes Peters, "Settler Forgetting in Saulnierville: The Sipekne'katik Mi'kmaw Fishery as Reminder," *Niche*, October 19, 2020. <https://niche-canada.org/2020/10/19/settler-forgetting-in-saulnierville-the-sipeknekatik-mikmaw-fishery-as-reminder/>.
5. For more information on the Boudreau case, see Megan Wennberg, writer and director, *The Killing of Phillip Boudreau*, CBC Docs, August 28, 2021. <https://www.cbc.ca/cbcdocspov/episodes/the-killing-of-phillip-boudreau>.
6. For more information on the Colton Boushie case, see Guy Quenneville, "What happened on Gerald Stanley's farm the day Colten Boushie was shot, as told by witnesses," *CBC News*, Feb 06, 2018. <https://www.cbc.ca/news/canada/saskatoon/what-happened-stanley-farm-boushie-shot-witnesses-colten-gerald-1.4520214>.

# Epilogue

Our circles are smaller now. There is less overlap between them.

It's almost five years—to the day—since Butcher killed Kristin.

Butcher lost his appeal. We don't need to talk about it. We all know.

Those of us who held each other down and through it all are all still here. We meet, after a year of lockdown, at a small restaurant on Quinpool Rd. in Halifax. We met here, at the same restaurant, the day before Kristin was killed.

I order a coffee and remember. We are older now. We are nursing babies and paying off debts for therapy we couldn't afford to live without.

I don't ever want to see Butcher again.

I have spent decades of my life with other killers, writing poems with them, advocating for programs and services for them, driving for hours to get to rural and remote prisons in the middle of godforsaken nowhere.

But this one is too close.

❧ ◇ ☙

In the United Kingdom, women protesting against violence during a vigil for Sarah Everard, the young woman who was killed by a cop, are beaten up by cops trying to break up the protest. They are being dragged away by cops in full tactical gear while media snap photos.[1]

The police in my town get an increase of $2.3 million dollars from last year's operating budget.

I have a board meeting coming up for a local sexual assault and healing centre. Some of our clients have been on a waitlist for months, trying to access counselling after a sexual assault.

Shanna Desmond's parents are still living in the home where the murders took place. No one wants to buy it. They have replaced the floors and tried to paint over the blood stains, but you can still see shadows behind the paint. They can't afford to move. Their grandchildren don't want to visit them there.[2]

☙◇❧

The server brings a round of coffee to the table.

I get an email on my phone from a man I know who was recently released from prison. He wants to start an organization helping men recover from violent behaviours. I promise to call him the following week to link him up with some folks who might be able to help.

I think about the night I got the phone call about Kristin's death.

I think about the courtroom artist from Butcher's trial. How he painted him, gaunt and sullen in his chair. One day, in the courthouse elevator, he told me that he can't walk through Halifax without seeing houses haunted by ghosts whose murderers he painted. He's spent decades painting portraits of the killers in my town. He tells me that, for him, the city is a map, riddled with memories from the stories he heard on the witness stand.

A friend makes eye contact from across the table, her green scarf vibrant and bold against her cheeks. "You okay?" she asks.

There is a stroller at the end of the table with a sleeping baby. Life is fucking precious.

I think about all the Aunties. All the ones who knew exactly what to do when shit hit the fan. All the insurgents who built systems of community accountability and healing justice while under constant threat of violence from kin and police.

I wonder if we will live up to them. I want to live up to them.

## Notes

1    Emma Graham-Harrison, "Police clash with mourners at Sarah Everard vigil in London, *Guardian*, March 13, 2021. <https://www.theguardian.com/uk-news/2021/mar/13/as-the-sun-set-they-came-in-solidarity-and-to-pay-tribute-to-sarah-everard>.

2.  See Aaron Beswick, "Family of Desmond murder-suicide victims can't escape crime scene," *Saltwire*, Sept. 26, 2019. <https://www.saltwire.com/nova-scotia/news/family-of-desmond-murder-suicide-victims-cant-escape-crime-scene-357217/>.

# Acknowledgements

In truth, this book should have a list of authors half a mile long. First and foremost, Kelly Donovan, Karyn Graham, Ivory Tuesday, Alok Mukherjee, Margot Van Sluytman and countless others who contributed to this book—thank you. I wish I could name all of you. Arthur Lockhart, your brilliance, deep wisdom and commitment to transformative justice has changed so many lives.

Thank you to Verona Singer; your mentorship and research had such a huge impact. Eulah Bent, who taught us about police violence and racism in our grade one class at Shelter Bay Elementary: God bless you. All children need a teacher like you. Janie Rozee, for your stories about Annie Mae Aquash and the FBI.

Thank you to all the frontline workers who possess deep knowledge about family violence and use this knowledge to save lives every day.

The references page should be placed here in the acknowledgements section. Without the work of abolitionist feminists and other precocious insurgents, we wouldn't have the language and tools we need to get *specific* and strategize together about abolition and domestic homicide.

Erin Wunker writes that in friendships, there are times *"where the intimacy and witnessing become too much for both for the world in which it exists and for the language of the world as it is."* It's hard to find the words to capture how certain friendships create space for building the unspeakable worlds that sustain us when everything else crumbles. El Jones, Cassie Thornton, Rosalynn Iuliucci, Bonnie Pero, Mark Gaspar: your wisdom and fire are what we need to burn it all down and build something beautiful. Max Haiven, Alex Khasnabish, Erin Wunker, Ajay Parasram, Margaret Campbell and Erin Fredericks, thank you for existing, resisting and making space for insurgence in the university.

Erin Steuter, Morgan Poteet, Fabrizio Antonelli, Christiana MacDougall and all our students in sociology at Mount Allison University, thank for you for being tireless co-conspirators and comrades in so many struggles for justice.

Fazeela Jiwa deserves special mention—I couldn't have finished this book without your solidarity, care and fantastic abolitionist imagination. Thank you to everyone at Fernwood Publishing and Emily Davidson for your contributions to this book. Candida Hadley, you made this book happen, too. Thank you. The Social Sciences and Humanities Research Council supported the research contained in these pages. Two reviewers contributed mightily to this book with generous and generative feedback. Thank you.

I must also thank Bert Knockwood, although this acknowledgement comes too late. Bert was murdered shortly before publication. Bert, if you're up there, spinning records in the sky, stop a moment and read this. Our conversations many years ago helped me to understand what healing can look like and how powerful it is when it happens. I am sorry I never got to tell you this in person. *Meskay nitap.* Rest in music.

Diem Saunders. My thank you comes too late to you, too. Thanks for being a mentor in grief; for making poetry out of the destruction and chaos that comes in the wake of a homicide. Rest in power. Rest in love. Rest in the knowledge that we will keep re-building the world for Kalluk. For you.

Finally, deep acknowledgement goes to Zachary Gough, for demonstrating how love and insurgence can mend what is broken and build what we need to survive. My conversations with you always made things feel clearer and less confusing. Love and thanks to you, papa Z, my beloved comrade in mischief and joyful rebellion.

# References

Abraham, Margaret, and Evangelia Tastsoglou. "Addressing Domestic Violence in Canada and the United States: Uneasy Co-habitation of Women and the State." *Current Sociology,* vol. 64, no. 4, 2016, pp. 568–585.

Alliance for Boys and Men of Color. "Healing Together." *Policy Link.* 2019. <https://allianceforbmoc.org/campaigns/healing-together>.

Amnesty International. "Police Violence." 2021. <https://www.amnesty.org/en/what-we-do/police-brutality/>.

Amor, Bani. "The Heart of Whiteness: On Spiritual Tourism and the Colonization of Ayahuasca." *Bitch Media,* 5 June 2019. <https://www.bitchmedia.org/article/heart-of-whiteness-spiritual-tourism-colonization-ayahuasca>.

Andersen, Jane, and Kimberly Christen. "Decolonizing Attribution: Traditions of Exclusion." *Journal of Radical Librarianship,* vol. 5, 2019, pp. 113–152.

Auchter, Bernie. "Men Who Murder Their Families: What the Research Tells Us." *National Institute of Justice Journal,* no. 266, 2010, pp. 10–12.

Barrie, Hannah. "No One Is Disposable: Towards Feminist Models of Transformative Justice." *Journal of Law and Social Policy,* vol. 33, no. 4, 2020, pp. 65–92.

Bashi, Vilna. "Globalized Anti-Blackness: Transnationalizing Western Immigration Law, Policy, and Practice." *Ethnic and Racial Studies,* vol. 27, no. 4, 2004, pp. 584–606. <DOI: 10.1080/01491987042000216726>.

Baskin, Cyndy. "Systematic Oppression, Violence, and Healing in Aboriginal Families and Communities." In Ramona Alaggia and Cathy Vine (eds.), *Cruel But Not Unusual: Violence in Canadian Families.* Wilfred Laurier University Press, 2012, p. 147–178.

Bazant, Micah, and Lewis Wallace. *Miklat Miklat.* Date unknown. <https://www.micahbazant.com/miklat-miklat>.

Beckett, Lois. "Teen Who Filmed George Floyd's Death Speaks Out: 'It Changed Me.'" *The Guardian,* 26 May 2021. <https://www.theguardian.com/us-news/2021/may/25/darnella-frazier-statement-george-floyd>.

Benson, Michael and Greer L. Fox. *Economic Distress, Community Context and Intimate Violence: An Application and Extension of Social Disorganization Theory, Final Report.* US Department of Justice, March 2002.

Berkin, Carol. "A Brief History of Women's History." *Saving Washington: Women and the American Story.* New York Historical Society Museum & Library, 2017.

Bierria, Alisa, Mimi Kim and Clarissa Rojas (eds.). "Community Accountability: Emerging Movements to Transform Violence." *Social Justice Journal,* vol. 37, no. 4, 2010.

Bird, Sharon. "Welcome to the Men's Club: Homosociality and the Maintenance of Hegemonic Masculinity." *Gender & Society,* vol. 10, no. 2, 1996. <https://psycnet.

apa.org/doi/10.1177/089124396010002002>.

Black, Bob. "The Abolition of Work." *The Anarchist Library*, 12 February 2009. <https://theanarchistlibrary.org/library/bob-black-the-abolition-of-work>.

Blackstock, Cindy. "Residential Schools: Did They Really Close or Just Morph into Child Welfare?" *Indigenous Law Journal,* vol. 6, no. 1, 2007, pp. 71–78.

Bousquet, Tim. "Lionel Desmond, His Tortured Soul, and His Guns: Morning File, Friday, January 6, 2017." *The Halifax Examiner*, 6 January 2017. <https://www.halifaxexaminer.ca/featured/lionel-desmond-his-tortured-soul-and-his-guns-morning-file-friday-january-6-2017/>.

brown, adrienne maree. *We Will Not Cancel Us and Other Dreams of Transformative Justice.* AK Press, 2020.

Bumiller, Kristin. *In an Abusive State: How Neoliberalism Appropriated the Feminist Movement Against Sexual Violence.* Duke University Press, 2008.

Butler, Paul. "Berkeley Talks Transcript: Paul Butler on How Prison Abolition Would Make Us All Safer." *Berkeley News*, 17 January 2020. <https://news.berkeley.edu/2020/01/17/berkeley-talks-transcript-paul-butler/>.

Campbell, Jacquelyn. "Danger Assessment" [Checklist Tool]. 2003. <https://www.dangerassessment.org/DATools.aspx>.

Campbell, Jacquelyn, et al. "Risk Factors for Femicide in Abusive Relationships: Results from a Multisite Case Control Study." *American Journal of Public Health,* vol. 93, no. 7, 2003, pp. 1089–1097. <https://dx.doi.org/10.2105%2Fajph.93.7.1089>.

Campbell, Marcie, et al. "Domestic Violence Risk Assessment: Informing Safety Planning & Risk Management." *Domestic Homicide Brief 2*. London, ON: Canadian Domestic Homicide Prevention Initiative, 2016a.

Campbell, Marcie et al. "Domestic Homicide Death Review Committees: Speaking for the Dead to Protect the Living." *Domestic Homicide Brief 1*. London, ON: Canadian Domestic Homicide Prevention Initiative, 2016b.

Canadian Press. "Protests Hit Val d'Or as Six Police Officers Not Charged for Alleged Abuse." *Toronto Star*, 18 November 2016. <https://www.thestar.com/news/canada/2016/11/18/protests-hit-val-dor-as-six-police-not-charged-for-alleged-abuse.html>.

___. "Desmond Inquiry: Psychologist Describes Former Soldier's Marital Difficulties." *Lethbridge News Now,* 25 February 2021. <https://lethbridgenewsnow.com/2021/02/25/desmond-inquiry-psychologist-describes-former-soldiers-marital-difficulties/>.

CCLA (Canadian Civil Liberties Association). "By the Numbers: Crime, Bail and Pre-Trial Detention in Canada." 2014.

Chartrand, Vicki. "Unsettled Times: Indigenous Incarceration and the Links between Colonialism and the Penitentiary in Canada." *Canadian Journal of Criminology and Criminal Justice*, vol. 61, no. 3, 2019, pp. 67–89.

Chen, Ching-In, Jai Dulani and Leah Lakshmi Piepzna-Samarasinha (eds.). *The Revolution Starts at Home: Confronting Intimate Violence Within Activist Communities.* AK Press, 2016.

Chrisjohn, Roland David, Sherri Young with Michael Maraun. *The Circle Game: Shadows and Substance in the Indian Residential School Experience in Canada.* Theytus Books, 1997. <https://www.researchgate.net/

publication/234625756_The_Circle_Game_Shadows_and_Substance_in_the_ Indian_Residential_School_Experience_in_Canada>.

Clancy, Devin. "Running the Fascists Out of Town: Then and Now." *Briarpatch Magazine*, 21 December 2017. <https://briarpatchmagazine.com/articles/view/ running-the-fascists-out-of-town>.

Conner, Kenneth, Catherine Ceruli and Eric Caine. "Threatened and Attempted Suicide by Partner-Violent Male Respondents Petitioned to Family Violence Court." *Violence and Victims,* vol. 17, no. 2, 2002, pp. 115–125.

Connolly, Amanda. "The Canadian Military Has Received More than 700 Sexual Assault Reports Since 2016: Data." Global News, 16 July 2021. <https://globalnews.ca/ news/8023284/canadian-forces-sexual-misconduct-tracking-ophtas/>.

Contenta, Sandro, et al. "CAS Study Reveals Stark Racial Disparities for Blacks, Aboriginals." *Toronto Star,* 23 June 2016. <https://www.thestar.com/news/canada/2016/06/23/ cas-study-reveals-stark-racial-disparities-for-blacks-aboriginals.html>.

Creative Interventions. "Creative Interventions Toolkit: A Practical Guide to Stop Interpersonal Violence." 2012. <www.creative-interventions.org/tools/toolkit/>._

Critical Resistance and Incite! "Critical Resistance-Incite! Statement on Gender Violence and the Prison-Industrial Complex." *Social Justice,* 30, 3, 141–150. 2003. <http:// www.jstor.org/stable/29768215>.

Crossman, Kimberly, Jennifer Hardesty and Marcela Raffaelli. "'He Could Scare Me Without Laying a Hand on Me': Mothers' Experiences of Nonviolent Coercive Control During Marriage and After Separation." *Violence Against Women*, vol. 22, no. 4, 2016, pp. 454–473.

Cuomo, Dana. "Domestic Violence, Abolitionism and the Problem of the Patriarchy." *Society and Space*, vol. 38, no. 6, 2020. <https://www.societyandspace.org/articles/ domestic-violence-abolitionism-and-the-problem-of-patriarchy>.

D'Souza, Steven. "Unprecedented: Gun and Ammunition Sales Spike Amid Coronavirus Spread." CBC News, 20 March 2020. <https://www.cbc.ca/news/world/unprecedented- gun-and-ammunition-sales-spike-amid-coronavirus-spread-1.5502092>.

Davis, Angela. "The Color of Violence Against Women." *Colorlines*, vol. 3, no. 3, 2000, pp. 4–8. <http://www.hartford-hwp.com/archives/45a/582.html>.

___. *Are Prisons Obsolete?* Seven Stories Press, 2003.

Dawson, Myrna. "Fatality and Death Reviews." *Homicide Studies*, vol. 17, no. 4, Nov. 2013, pp. 335–338.

___. "Punishing Femicide: Criminal Justice Responses to the Killing of Women over Four Decades." *Current Sociology*, vol. 64, no. 7, 2015. <https://doi.org/10.1177 %2F0011392115611192>.

Dixon, Ejeris, and Leah Lakshmi Piepzna-Samarasinha. *Beyond Survival: Strategies and Stories from the Transformative Justice Movement.* AK Press, 2020.

Dobash, Emmerson, R., and Russell Dobash. *Violence against Wives: A Case against Patriarchy.* Free Press, 1979.

Donovan, Catherine, and Rebecca Barnes. *Queering Narratives of Domestic Violence and Abuse: Victims and/or Perpetrators?* Palgrave Pivot, 2020.

Dutton, Donald, and Greg Kerry. "Modus Operandi and Personality Disorder in Incarcerated Spousal Killers." *International Journal of Law and Psychiatry*, vol. 22, no. 3–4, 1999, pp. 287–299.

Dworkin, Andrea. *Woman Hating*. Dutton, 1974.

Fanon, Frantz. *The Wretched of the Earth*. Grove Press, 1963.

Flood, Michael. "Men, Sex, and Homosociality: How Bonds between Men Shape Their Sexual Relations with Women." *Men and Masculinities,* vol. 10, no. 3, 2007, pp. 339–359. <https://doi.org/10.1177/1097184X06287761>.

Fraser, Jennifer. "Claims-making In Context: Forty Years of Canadian Feminist Activism on Violence Against Women." Thesis submitted to FGS, University of Ottawa Department of Criminology. 2014

Frayne, David. *The Refusal of Work: The Theory, Practice and Resistance to Work*. Zed Books, 2015.

Fridel, Emma E., and James Alan Fox. "Gender Differences in Patterns and Trends in US Homicide 1976–2017." In *Violence and Gender,* vol. 6, no. 1, 2019, pp. 27–36. <http://doi.org/10.1089/vio.2019.0005 2019>.

Generation Five. *Toward Transformative Justice: A Liberatory Approach to Child Sexual Abuse and Other Forms of Intimate and Community Violence*. Generation Five, 2007. <http://www.generationfive.org/wp-content/uploads/2013/07/G5_Toward_Transformative_Justice-Document.pdf>.

Gerster, Jane. "More Men Are Killed than Women so Why Focus on Violence Against Women?" *Global News Canada*. 22 February 2020. <https://globalnews.ca/news/6536184/gender-based-violence-men-women/>.

Gilio-Whitaker, Dina. "The Problem with the Ecological Indian Stereotype." *KCET*, 7 February 2017. <https://www.kcet.org/shows/tending-the-wild/the-problem-with-the-ecological-indian-stereotype>.

Goodmark, Leigh. *Decriminalizing Domestic Violence: A Balanced Policy Approach to Intimate Partner Violence*. University of California Press, 2018.

Gouldhawke, Mike. "A Condensed History of Canada's Colonial Cops: How the RCMP Has Secured the Imperialist Power of the North." *The New Inquiry*, 10 March, 2020. <https://thenewinquiry.com/a-condensed-history-of-canadas-colonial-cops/>.

Hahn, Miriam. "Playing Hippies and Indians: Acts of Cultural Colonization in the Theatre of American Counterculture." PhD dissertation, Bowling Green State University. 2014. <https://scholarworks.bgsu.edu/theatre_diss/5>.

Hartman, Saidiya. *Scenes of Subjection: Terror, Slavery and Self-Making in Nineteenth-Century America*. Oxford University Press, 1997.

___. "On Insurgent Histories and the Abolitionist Imaginary." *Art Forum*. 14 July 2020. <https://www.artforum.com/interviews/saidiya-hartman-83579>.

Helmore, Edward. "US Gun Sales Spiked During Pandemic and Continue to Rise." *The Guardian,* 31 May 2021. <https://www.theguardian.com/us-news/2021/may/31/us-gun-sales-rise-pandemic>.

Hernández, Kelly Lytle. *City of Inmates: Conquest, Rebellion, and the Rise of Human Caging in Los Angeles, 1771–1965*. University of North Carolina Press, 2017.

hooks, bell. *All About Love: New Visions*. HarperCollins, 2018.

Incite! *Color of Violence: The Incite! Anthology*. Duke University Press, 2016.

Incite! & Critical Resistance. "Statement on Gender-Based Violence and the Prison Industrial Complex." 2001. <https://incite-national.org/incite-critical-resistance-statement/>.

Jaffe, Peter, Katreena Scott and Anna-Lee Straatman (eds.). *Preventing Domestic Homicides:*

*Lessons Learned from Tragedies.* Academic Press, 2020.

James, Llana. "Censure and Silence: Sexual Violence and Women of the African Diaspora." In Notisha Massaquoi and Njoki Nathani Wane (eds.), *Theorizing Empowerment: Canadian Perspectives on Black Feminist Thought.* Inanna Publications and Education, 2007, pp. 228–244.

Jeffrey, N., Fairbairn, J., Campbell, M., Dawson, M., Jaffe, P. & Straatman, A-L. Canadian Domestic Homicide Prevention Initiative with Vulnerable Populations (CDHPIVP) Literature Review on Risk Assessment, Risk Management and Safety Planning. London, ON: Canadian Domestic Homicide Prevention Initiative. November 2018.

Johnson, Michael. "Patriarchal Terrorism and Common Couple Violence: Two Forms of Violence Against Women." *Journal of Marriage and Family,* vol. 57, no. 2, 1995, pp. 283–294.

___. *A Typology of Domestic Violence: Intimate Terrorism, Violent Resistance, and Situational Couple Violence.* Northeastern University Press, 2008.

Johnson, Michael, and Kathleen Ferraro. "Research on Domestic Violence in the 1990s: Making Distinctions." *Journal of Marriage and the Family,* vol. 62, no. 4, 2000, pp. 948–963.

Kaba, Mariame. "Yes, We Mean Literally Abolish the Police." *New York Times,* 12 June 2020, <https://www.nytimes.com/2020/06/12/opinion/sunday/floyd-abolish-defund-police.html>.

___. *We Do This 'Till We Free Us: Abolitionist Organizing and Transforming Justice.* Haymarket Books, 2021.

Kaba, Mariame, and Shira Hassan. *Fumbling Towards Repair: A Workbook for Community Accountability Facilitators.* Project NIA/Just-Practice, 2019.

Kim, Mimi. "From Carceral Feminism to Transformative Justice: Women-of-Color Feminism and Alternatives to Incarceration." *Journal of Ethnic and Cultural Diversity in Social Work,* vol. 27, no. 3, 2018, pp. 219–233.

Kivisto, Aaron. "Male Perpetrators of Intimate Partner Homicide: A Review and Proposed Typology." *The Journal of the American Academy of Psychiatry and the Law,* vol. 43, no. 3, 2015, pp. 300–312.

Kurz, Demie. "Social Science Perspectives on Wife Abuse: Current Debates and Future Directions." *Gender & Society,* vol. 3, no. 4, 1989, pp. 489–505.

Lagerquist, Jeffery. "Calgary Police Link Domestic Violence Spike to Economic Downturn." *CTV News,* May 18, 2016. <https://www.ctvnews.ca/canada/calgary-police-link-domestic-violence-spike-to-economic-downturn-1.2908381>.

Lalonde, Julie. *Resilience Is Futile: The Life and Death of Julie Lalonde.* Between the Lines, 2020.

Law, Victoria. "Against Carceral Feminism." *Jacobin,* 17 October, 2014. <https://www.jacobinmag.com/2014/10/against-carceral-feminism/>.

Lockhart, Arthur, and Lynn Zammit. *Restorative Justice: Transforming Society.* Inclusion Press, 2005.

MacKinnon, Catharine. *Feminism Unmodified.* Harvard University Press, 1987.

Malone, Kelly Geraldine, et al. "Police Shootings in 2020: The Effect on Officers and Those They Are Sworn to Protect." *CBC News,* 21 December 2020. <https://www.cbc.ca/news/canada/manitoba/police-shootings-2020-yer-review-1.5849788>.

Maynard, Robyn. *Policing Black Lives: State Violence in Canada from Slavery to Present.*

Fernwood Publishing, 2017.

McEvoy, Claire and Gergely Hideg. *Global Violent Deaths 2017: Time to Decide*. Small Arms Survey, 2017. <http://www.smallarmssurvey.org/fileadmin/docs/U-Reports/SAS-Report-GVD2017.pdf>.

The Men's Project and Michael Flood. *Unpacking the Man Box: What Is The Impact of the Man Box Attitudes on Young Australian Men's Behaviours and Wellbeing?* Jesuit Social Services, 2020. <https://jss.org.au/what-we-do/the-mens-project/unpacking-the-man-box/>.

Merivale, Herman. *Lectures on Colonization and the Colonies: Lectures delivered at the University of Oxford 1839, 1849 & 1841*. Longman, Green, Longman and Roberts, 1861.

Moreton-Robinson, Aileen. *The White Possessive: Property, Power and Indigenous Sovereignty*. University of Minnesota Press, 2015.

Morris, Ruth. *Stories of Transformative Justice*. Canadian Scholars Press, 2000.

Mukherjee, A., and Harper, T. *Excessive Force: Toronto's Fight to Reform City Policing*. Douglas and McIntyre, 2018.

Natapoff, Alexandra. "Underenforcement." *Fordham Law Review*, vol. 75, no. 3, 2006, pp. 1715–1776.

National Cancer Institute. "Survivorship." *National Institutes of Health Cancer Dictionary*. <https://www.cancer.gov/publications/dictionaries/cancer-terms/def/survivorship>.

National Coalition Against Domestic Violence. "Domestic Violence." 2020. <https://assets.speakcdn.com/assets/2497/domestic_violence-2020080709350855.pdf?1596811079991>.

NCTE (National Centre for Transgender Equality). "2015 Transgender Survey Report." 2015. <https://vawnet.org/material/2015-us-transgender-survey-report>.

Nocella, Anthony J. "An Overview of the History and Theory of Transformative Justice." *Peace & Conflict Review*. 6:1. 2011.

Page, Julia. "Reports Indigenous Women Were Abused by Retired Police Officer Never Led to Charges, Viens Commission Hears." CBC News Canada, 16 August 2018. <https://www.cbc.ca/news/canada/montreal/alleged-sexual-assault-police-val-d-or-viens-commission-1.4788002>.

Palacios, L.C. "'Something Else to Be': A Chicana Survivor's Journey from Vigilante Justice to Transformative Justice." *Philosophia*, vol. 6, no. 1, p[p. 93–108, 2016.

Palmater, Pam. "Canada Should Declassify, Deconstruct and Defund the RCMP." *Canadian Dimension,* 15 June 2020. <https://canadiandimension.com/articles/view/declassify-deconstruct-and-defund-the-rcmp>.

___. "Shining Light on the Dark Places: Addressing Police Racism and Sexualized Violence against Indigenous Women and Girls in the National Inquiry." *Canadian Journal of Women and the Law*, vol. 28, no. 2, 2016, pp. 253–284.

Philpart, Marc. "Healing, not Policing: A Transformative Approach to Intimate Partner Violence." Alliance for Men and Boys of Color. Issue No 28. October 28, 2020 < https://allianceforbmoc.org/covid19-and-race/healing-not-policing>.

Richardson/Kinewesquao, Catherine, Ann Maje Rader, Barbara McInerney, Renee-Claude Carrier. "Creating Safety and Justice for Women In the Yukon." In *Social Justice and Counselling* , 2017.

Richie, Beth. *Arrested Justice: Black Women, Violence, and America's Prison Nation*. New York University Press, 2012.

Robinson, Cedric. *Black Marxism: The Making of a Black Radical Tradition*. University of North Carolina Press, 2000.

Russo, Ann. *Feminist Accountability: Disrupting Violence and Transforming Power*. New York University Press, 2018.

Ryan, Cary, et al. "A Review of Pro-Arrest, Pro-Charge, and Pro-Prosecution Policies as a Response to Domestic Violence." *Journal of Social Work*, vol. 21, no. 1, 2021.

Saleh-Hanna, Viviane. "Black Feminist Hauntology." Champ Pénal/Penal Field [En ligne], vol. XII | 2015, mis en ligne le 17 février 2016, consulté le 28 juillet 2021. <https://doi.org/10.4000/champpenal.9168>.

Sawyer, Wendy, and Peter Wagner. "Mass Incarceration: The Whole Pie 2020 Report." Prison Policy Initiative. 24 March 2020. <https://www.prisonpolicy.org/reports/pie2020.html>.

Schenwar, Maya, and Victoria Law. *Prison by Any Other Name: The Harmful Consequences of Popular Reforms*. The New Press, 2020.

Schneider, Daniel, Kristen Harknett and Sara McLanahan. "Intimate Partner Violence in the Great Recession." *Demography*, vol. 53, no. 2, 2016, pp. 471–505.

Sharpe, Christina. "Lose Your Kin" In *The New Inquiry*. https://thenewinquiry.com/lose-your-kin/ 2016.

Sheehy, E.A. "Legal Responses to Violence." *Canadian Women's Studies*, vol. 19, 1999, 1–2.

Shotwell, Alexis. "Claiming Bad Kin." 2 March, 2018. <https://alexisshotwell.com/2018/03/02/claiming-bad-kin/>.

Simpson, Leanne Betasamosake. *As We Have Always Done: Indigenous Freedom Through Radical Resistance*. University of Minnesota Press, 2017.

Singer, Verona. "Tensions in the Dominant Domestic Violence Discourse and the High Risk Case Coordination Protocol." 2012. PhD dissertation, Dalhousie University.

Singh, Inayat. "2020 Already a Particularly Deadly Year for People Killed in Police Encounters, CBC Research Shows." *CBC News*, 23 July 2020. <https://newsinteractives.cbc.ca/fatalpoliceencounters/>.

SPTDC (Stop Police Terror Project DC). "No More Stop and Frisk." 2021. <https://www.sptdc.com/nomorestopandfrisk>.

Stark, Evan. *Coercive Control: How Men Entrap Women in Personal Life*. Oxford University Press, 2009.

Statistics Canada. "Homicide in Canada, 2014." Statistics Canada Catalogue no. 85-002-X ISSN 1209-6393. *Canadian Centre for Justice Statistics*, 25 November 2014. <https://www150.statcan.gc.ca/n1/pub/85-002-x/2015001/article/14244-eng.htm>.

Steinmetz, Suzanne. "Battered Husband Syndrome." *Victimology*, vol. 2, no. 3/4, 1977, pp. 499–509.

Stretton, Tim. and Krista J. Kesselring. *Married Women and the Law: Coverture in England and the Common Law World*. McGill-Queen's University Press, 2013.

Szalavitz, Maia. "Income Inequality's Most Disturbing Side Effect: Homicide." *Scientific American*, 1 November 2018. <https://www.scientificamerican.com/article/income-inequalitys-most-disturbing-side-effect-homicide/>.

Tallbear, Kim. "Making Love and Relations, Beyond Settler Sex & Family" In Adele Clark, and Donna Haraway(eds.), *Making Kin not Population*. Prickly Paradigm Press, 2018.

Tauri, Juan Marcellus. "Indigenous Peoples and the Globalization of Restorative Justice." *Social Justice,* vol. 43, no. 3, 2016, pp. 46–67.

Third Eye Collective. "Who We Are." n.d. <https://thirdeyecollective.wordpress.com/about/>.

Tulloch, Michael (The Honorable Justice). *Report of the Independent Police Oversight Review.* Queen's Printer for Ontario, 2017, <https://www.attorneygeneral.jus.gov. on.ca/english/about/pubs/police_oversight_review/>.

Undercommoning Collective. "Undercommoning within, against and beyond the university-as-such." In *Roar Mag.* June 5th, 2016. <https://roarmag.org/essays/ undercommoning-collective-university-education/>.

UN Human Rights Office of the High Commissioner. "Femicide Watch Initiative." 2021. <https://www.ohchr.org/en/issues/women/srwomen/pages/femicidewatch.aspx>.

Velopulos, C. G., Carmichael, H., Zakrison, T. L., & Crandall, M. "Comparison of Male and Female Victims of Intimate Partner Homicide and Bidirectionality: An Analysis of the National Violent Death Reporting System." *The Journal of Trauma and Acute Care Surgery*, vol. 87, no. 2, 2019, pp 331–336. <https://doi.org/10.1097/ TA.0000000000002276>.

Vitale, Alex. *The End of Policing.* Verso Books, 2017.

Wacquant, Loic. *Prisons of Poverty.* University of Minnesota Press, 2009.

Walcott, Rinaldo. *On Property.* Biblioasis, 2021.

Warren, Rosie and Yasmin Nair. "The Political Is Political: In Conversation with Yasmin Nair." Salvage, 25 July 2016. <https://salvage.zone/in-print/ the-political-is-political-in-conversation-with-yasmin-nair/>.

Websdale, Neil. *Familicidal Hearts: The Emotional Styles of 211 Killers.* Oxford University Press, 2010.

Weeks, Kathi. *The Problem with Work: Feminism, Marxism, Antiwork Politics and Postwork Imaginaries.* Duke University Press, 2011.

Whynacht, Ardath. "Prison in the Spaces Between Us: Abolition, Austerity, and the Possibility of Compassionate Containments." In Alex Khasnabish and Max Haiven (eds.), *What Moves Us: The Lives and Times of the Radical Imagination.* Fernwood Publishing and Upping the Anti, 2017.

Whynacht Ardath, Emily Arsenault, and Rachael Conney,. "Abolitionist Pedagogy in the Neoliberal University." *Social Justice Journal* 45: 4. 2018.

WILPF (Women's International League for Peace and Freedom). "The Invisible Epidemic of Police Violence against Women." 4 January 2021. <https://www.wilpf.org/ the-invisible-epidemic-of-police-violence-against-women/>.

Wilson, Robin, Franca Cortoni, and Andrew J. McWhinnie. *Circles of Support & Accountability: A Canadian National Replication of Outcome Findings.* The Association for the Treatment of Sexual Abusers. 2009. <https://doi. org/10.1177/1079063209347724>.

Wilson Gilmore, Ruthie. *Golden Gulag: Prisons, Surplus, Crisis, and Opposition in Globalizing California.* University of California Press, 2007.

Withers, AJ. *Transformative Justice and/as Harm.* Rebuild Printing, 2014.

Young, Tuma. "L'nuwita'simk A Foundational Worldview for a L'nuwey Justice System." *Indigenous Law Journal,* vol. 11, no. 1, 2016, pp. 75–102.

# Index

abolition, 123–24
  accountability circles, *see* accountability
  as Black movement, 23–24
  building support for, 2, 15–16, 23, 26–29, 117
  community strategies and, 98–111, 115–16
  definition of, 12, 29
  disposability and, 87, 118–20, 129
  domestic homicide and, 42–43, 65, 87–88, 127
  feminism and, *see* abolitionist feminism
  harm and, 85–88, 98, 102, 118–19
  incarcerated people's involvement, 25, 85–87, 92, 111
  logic of, 11–17, 20–22, 26–28, 50, 97, 117
  occupational stress and, 73, 87–88, 101, 127
  police, 2, 54–58, 98–99, 127
  prisons, 2, 29, 111
  transformative justice and, 19–23, 56, 98–99, 115, 127
  white settlers and, 21–26, 97, 109, 118, 127
  writing on, 6, 11, 19, 42, 50, 108–9, 122
  youth and, *see* youth
abolitionist feminism,
  Black, 15, 23, 107
  logic of, 2, 12–16, 20, 22, 100, 107, 118
  need for, 15–16, 23, 26, 134
  types of violence and, 2, 42, 116
  *see also* abolition
abuse, 14, 98, 101
  accountability for, *see* accountability
  boundary-crossing, 43–44, 76, 85, 107, 119, 121, 129
  child, 8, 49, 52, 69–70, 76, 83, 92, 108–10, 125
  dismissing, 18, 27, 33–35, 41, 50, 82–86, 90
  elder, 8–9, 27, 109–10
  high-risk, 10, 40–43, 74, 81–82, 87, 103–6
  occupational stress and, 75, 77, 84, 88, 101; *see also* occupational stress
  online, 3, 46, 69
  by police, 14, 52–58, 61–62, 103–4, 114
  racialized communities and, 14–15, 48–50, 55–57, 110

  red flags for, *see* red flags
  sexual, *see* sexual abuse
  types of, 42–50, 100–2, 108–10
  unexpected, 3, 81–82
abusers,
  antisocial, 81–82
  collective self-defence against, *see* collective self-defence
  emotionally dependent, 81–82, 107–8
  fleeing from, 4, 32, 43, 95
  grooming, 2, 71, 80–81
  insurgent collaboration with, 98, 126–29, 132
  as kin, 33, 76, 84, 121–23, 126
  logic of, 40–41, 58–62, 70, 74–76, 105–6, 111–12; *see also* possession
  possessiveness of, *see* possession
  protection from, 12, 42–49, 104–9, 112–14, 117–18, 126
  relationships with, 10, 17–18, 84–87, 95, 118–20
  reporting, 1, 17, 36, 93, 98–99, 105, 110, 125
  retaliation of, 1, 61–62, 66–67, 101, 112
  settler, 112–13
  societal perceptions of, 11–12, 14, 64, 81–86, 111–12
  stereotypes of, 18, 82
  support programs for, 64–65, 83–87, 103, 108–9, 116–18, 131
  surrogate, 122–23, 126
  threats of, 7, 32, 38, 51–52, 104–7, 112
accountability,
  absolving of, 32–33, 82
  circles, 25–26, 42, 98, 100, 109
  community, 51, 100–2, 105–9, 121–23, 126, 132
  desire to take, 18, 35, 85, 109
  evading, 18, 25, 102–3, 112, 116
  seeking abuser, 56, 65, 85, 91–92, 116–19
  societal, 18–19, 56, 87
  support with, 35, 79, 92, 109, 116–20
addiction, 29, 44, 51, 91, 103, 113; *see also* substance use
advocacy, 47, 53, 67, 114
  abolition, 20, 85, 108–9, 119–20, 123–24, 131
  critiques of, 10–11, 23, 97
  survivors, working with, 1, 5, 24–25, 43,